K2: The Price of Conquest

K2: THE PRICE OF CONQUEST

Lino Lacedelli & Giovanni Cenacchi

(Translated by Mark Worthington)

CARREG
THE MOUNTAINEERS BOOKS

First published in 2006 in Great Britain by
Carreg Limited
18 Parsons Croft
Hildersley, Ross-on-Wye
Herefordshire   HR9 5BN

Published simultaneously in the United States of America by

The Mountaineers Books
1001 SW Klickitat Way
Suite 201
Seattle, WA 98134

Text © Giovanni Cenacchi 2006
Photos © Lino Lacedelli 2006

Lino Lacedelli dedicates this book to Mario Puchoz.

Giovanni Cenacchi dedicates this book to Viola.

Lino Lacedelli in 1954.

Contents

Part 1

Before Lacedelli

Why we should believe Lino Lacedelli

For many reasons, it is difficult today to doubt the words of Lino Lacedelli. The main reason is that he was actually there and witnessed the events himself, but another is because of the long silence that he has maintained.

On his return from the successful expedition in the autumn of 1954, Lacedelli, together with his summit companion Achille Compagnoni, signed the 'official' report on the expedition, which had been published by Ardito Desio[*]. After that, from Lino Lacedelli, there was almost nothing but silence. He limited his public appearances to the usual official engagements, and to the most prestigious award ceremonies. On each of these occasions his statements were brief and hesitant, despite the media interest surrounding the expedition, particularly regarding the two mountaineers who had reached the summit.

The conquest of K2 gave the Italian nation a period of euphoria that is difficult to understand, until it is remembered that not many years had passed since the end of the Second World War. With this mountaineering triumph Italy was able, for the first time, to raise proudly its flag over the debris of humiliation and defeat. Today mountaineering is part of the Italian consciousness (in part undoubtedly because of what happened on K2 fifty years ago), though mountaineers often complain about the superficial way in which the activity is covered in newspapers and television. That is not new: Lacedelli, on his return, had to put up with articles in

---

[*] Ardito Desio, *La Conquista del K2*, Garzanti, Milano, 1954 (the same publisher produced a new edition in 2004). Published in English as *Ascent of K2*, Elek Books Ltd, 1955.

which K2 was said to be short for 'Kilometre 2', and that an exhausted Lino Lacedelli had been dragged to the top of the mountain by Achille Compagnoni. Lacedelli handled the errors, spiteful words and insinuations with dignity. He avoided getting embroiled in the denials and arguments, even to the point of hiding himself away in the hayloft of his house in Cortina d'Ampezzo whenever journalists came to interview him.

The passing of the years saw a deterioration in the relationship between the K2 expedition and the media. Walter Bonatti, who, the night before the final ascent, had risked his life carrying the oxygen bottles needed for the final climb to Lacedelli and Compagnoni, was accused in 1964, by the journalist Nino Giglio in *Nuova Gazzetta del Popolo*, of having tried to 'steal' the triumph from Lacedelli and Compagnoni. He was also accused of having abandoned the porter who had accompanied him to a tragic fate, and of himself using some of the oxygen required by the two summit climbers. Bonatti had been feeling victimised up to that day. The evening before the final ascent, finding himself with the porter Mahdi at more than 8,000 metres, not finding Camp IX in the place he assumed it to be, and without assistance by Lacedelli and Compagnoni, he was forced to endure a terrible night in the open without equipment.

Bonatti began a libel suit against Nino Giglio, and launched an angry offensive against Ardito Desio and the Lacedelli-Compagnoni combination by writing a book. Although Achille Compagnoni was the immediate target for Bonatti's attack (Nino Giglio had declared in court that most of the information in his articles had come from Compagnoni), mud was also thrown in Lacedelli's direction, although the latter didn't seem particularly concerned.

Lino Lacedelli was not present at the hearing, which was won by Bonatti, nor did he concern himself, prior to this present book, with clarifying his role in, or giving his view of, the events of that terrible night at the end of July 1954. The years which followed the trial were littered with attempts to revise the story, these generally degenerating into new arguments, ambiguous silences and skirmishes with the newspapers. Again, Lino Lacedelli made an effort to stay above it all. He preferred the peace of the mountains to the noise of the crowds, glory without fame.

It may be a digression but perhaps the paradox of glory without fame is typical of the mind of the mountaineer. In any case, the fact that Lacedelli today feels the need to tell the truth about what happened is not because he has to. The necessity to refute insinuations and insults should have been stronger in previous years, the years in which he preferred to remain silent. This need seems to be the fruit of a free will and a serene mind. It comes from a desire, from a man on the threshold of his eightieth birthday, for clarity on a page of history which has not, to this point, been described with complete objectivity. Added to this is a desire that the evidence of one of the main players in the expedition should not be allowed to disappear into oblivion: to signal a new call for justice by clarifying the many, often incorrect, accounts of the expedition; and to set down a true account on behalf of the many other silent participants, the climbers, the majority of whom followed Lacedelli's example, talking little and declining to get involved in the arguments. They are the mountaineers who climbed K2 first, but for fifty years the story of that expedition has not been their story: on that subject there is still much to tell.

'I never said these things, because we couldn't say them'

Another reason for believing what Lacedelli says today, and at the same time explaining his silence at the time, arises from the role that he played on the K2 expedition. Lacedelli, as he will say himself many times in the following pages, felt he was actually little more than a porter. Although he had an excellent mountaineering pedigree, the role he was given by Ardito Desio required him, from the beginning, to do a lot of fetching and carrying. Lacedelli felt that there was a prejudice, always denied in the official history, against climbers from the Dolomites, a view that they were less capable of dealing with the extreme conditions of the Himalayan and Karakoram mountains. Other excellent climbers from the Dolomites, such as Soldà and Abram, were given the same treatment.

Added to this feeling of injustice was the decision by Ardito Desio, who seemed to fear the presence of mountaineers who were too famous or had too strong a personality, to exclude Riccardo Cassin for medical reasons, reasons so tenuous as to border on the comical. Cassin was the first victim of Desio's egotism. Ardito Desio, who was a great organiser and seemed successful at building relationships in the early phase of the expedition, later proved to be an inadequate leader. His insensitivity towards the climbers, the arbitrary way in which he issued orders, and his authoritarianism without authority, created a near-impossible situation. The summit was reached in an atmosphere of 'silent mutiny' that allowed the climbers, in Desio's absence from the heart of the action high on the Abruzzi Spur, a certain amount of autonomy. It was certainly not part of Desio's plans that Lacedelli should reach the summit, and the mutual embarrassment it caused was obvious following the return of the expedition to Italy. Desio, who, during the preparations for the expedition, had done everything he could to build up his own profile, could not tolerate the quiet, proud mountaineer who had stolen the limelight from him. In contrast to Compagnoni, Lacedelli, who already had an impressive climbing record before the K2 expedition, did not meekly accept Desio's decisions, even when they seemed absurd, sided with his fellow climbers when there were disagreements, and felt no obligation towards Desio after the expedition had left Base Camp for Italy.

On the expedition's return to Italy Lacedelli found himself a star member of an expedition in which he felt he had struggled to establish himself, until the final climb. Desio, an able manipulator of his own public image, wasted no time in putting himself on show. For Lacedelli, celebrating the Italian expedition required magnifying the image of its leader, a man for whom he had little regard.

Back in Italy, Ardito Desio did nothing to reduce the tension existing between himself and the mountaineers. He accused the cameraman Mario Fantin of having stolen some reels of film, despite one of the members of the scientific expedition owning up to having removed them in good faith. He continued to state that the scientific achievements of the expedition were as valuable, if not more so, than the mountaineering achievements. As a result of this, in January 1955 a letter was sent to the Executive Committee for K2 of the CAI (Italian Alpine Club) expressing general dissatisfaction with the expedition. It was signed by all the team members except Compagnoni and Viotto. This letter followed one which had been sent to the same Committee the previous December by Ugo Angelino (whom Desio had nominated as his second-in-command) expressing serious concerns about Desio's behaviour.

But although these tensions leaked out occasionally into the gossip columns of the Italian press, the general population, caught up in a sense of patriotic pride and in need of national heroes, took little notice. At that time (the early 1950s) mountaineering expeditions to the high peaks of the Himalayas and Karakoram engendered a strong sense of nationalism, despite the fact that in the year before the K2 expedition, John Hunt, the leader of the British

Everest expedition and himself an extremely capable mountaineer, was willing to carry loads to 8,350 metres and then allow a Nepalese Sherpa and a New Zealander to be the first to reach the summit. All the embarrassment, and the understanding of 'how it really was', was of no help to the by-now famous mountaineers. Apart from discussions behind closed doors within CAI, which didn't exert real authority over Desio, this little group of romantic heroes were given no space to re-establish the truth of a story that had already been written without investigation.

For the shy and retiring Lacedelli, the role of national hero did not come easy. If he had raised his voice and contradicted the official report, he would have been squashed by Desio, who had already tried to seize the private photos and diaries belonging to the climbers. He had also forced them to sign a 'discipline agreement' which gave him, as leader, the sole right of publication on, and communication about, the expedition. As an example of the powerful influence exerted by Desio, despite the fact that from the 4 August 1954 articles and photos heralding the success of the expedition had started to appear on the front pages of Italy's national press, only on the 12 October were the names of Lacedelli and Compagnoni released. The official reason was to avoid any individuals receiving an unequal share of the plaudits. In reality, the release of the names followed Desio's late return to Italy, and was a result of his insistence that responsibility for all communications was his alone.

When the climbers finally felt themselves free to give their own versions of events it was too late. There were already debates in the press and disputes in the courts – Compagnoni against the CAI, the CAI against Desio, Bonatti against Nino Giglio. To add their voices to the general uproar would have merely added to the confusion. The man who had suffered most in the years that followed the expedition, Walter Bonatti, has continued to fan the flames of controversy, right up to the present day. In the light of that history, when would it have been appropriate for Lacedelli to talk? His response to this question was 'as late as possible'. Taking advantage of the 50th anniversary certainly, but also ensuring the maximum length of time from the expedition so that he could not be accused of being motivated by personal interest or in the settling of old accounts.

Today, Lino Lacedelli can speak with the freedom and authority of someone who has no need to defend or accuse anyone. He has never orchestrated the media circus, as some have, or, like Bonatti, been involved in a continuous struggle since 1954. Though the bookshops are full of accounts of the expedition, fifty years of distance provide the most convincing proof of his detachment and honesty. Certainly, in all these years, some have suffered a great deal because of wrong historical accounts. Walter Bonatti's role, in particular, a role which has probably aroused the most discussion, has now been confirmed definitively by Lacedelli. He explains things that Bonatti was only able to hint at, as, for example, the events surrounding the position of Camp IX. On the other hand, Lacedelli refutes Bonatti's theory about the oxygen running out before he (Lacedelli) and Compagnoni arrived at the summit. These are only two of the many episodes that Lacedelli's testimony reveals, throwing light on the several omissions from the official story. These episodes give an account of the true roles of the other climbers, roles which have never been fully appreciated. The suffering, lack of recognition and togetherness of the climbers provide a backdrop to the stories, which the history of mountaineering must sooner or later acknowledge. Lino Lacedelli, with the interview that follows, has finally had his say.

A Brief History of the Exploration of K2 and a Chronological Account of the 1954 Italian Expedition

K2, known locally as Chogori, has often been called 'The Italian Mountain', not only because the Italian flag was planted on its summit on the 31st of July 1954, but also because it had, over the years, attracted an unusually large number of Italians, who came to admire, measure and attempt it, in the years before the expedition of 1954.

The great pyramid of K2 was first identified (by theodolite) in 1856, during Colonel T.G. Montgomery's Survey of India, a survey undertaken as part of the exploration and recording of the remotest parts of the British Empire. The peak was first registered as N13, but later this was changed to K2 (the second peak of the Karakoram to be classified, after Masherbrum, which was K1). In 1861, Henry H. Godwin-Austen, the Survey's topographer, identified the mountain for the first time with the naked eye. A number of explorers (such as Martin Conway), geographers and soldiers (such as Francis Younghusband, the leader of several spectacular expeditions to high and remote areas) visited the area close to the mountain in subsequent years. Particularly noteworthy was the visit of the explorer Roberto Lerco, from Val d'Aosta, who reached K2's lower slopes in 1890.

One of the first attempts on the peak was led by HRH Luigi Amedeo of the House of Savoy, Duke of the Abruzzi, who in the spring of 1909, led an assorted group of climbers and Italian scholars, aided by 350 local porters, on a detailed exploration of the approaches to the mountain. The expedition identified the southeast spur as the best route to the summit, confirming the view of the English mountaineer, and practitioner of the occult, Aleister Crowley who had reached the mountain's base in 1892. The Duke's expedition reached no higher than 6,000 metres on the spur, which has subsequently become known as the Abruzzi Spur, and was the chosen ascent route in 1954.

Though failing to gain appreciable height on K2, the Duke's expedition achieved many noteworthy results. The climbers also attempted Chogolisa (Bride Peak): they failed to reach the summit by only 150 metres, but the new world record altitude they achieved proved that, contrary to then current scientific predictions, it was possible to survive for days above 6,000 metres. The 1:75,000 map drawn up by the naval captain, the Marquis Federico Negrotto, became the basis for future cartography. The report written by the expedition doctor Filippo de Filippi was equally valuable, and the extraordinary photographs taken by the photographer/textile industrialist/landowner/banker Vittorio Sella guaranteed the immortality of the expedition. His images of the Baltoro Glacier and his panoramas of the Karakoram are probably the most famous mountain photographs ever taken. Sella was also the first to use a movie camera on a mountaineering expedition.

After the Duke of the Abruzzi's expedition, many years passed before the Italians came back to K2. An expedition was planned in 1929 by the CAI and the Italian Geographical Society, but the tragedy that overtook Umberto Nobile and his airship over the North Pole persuaded Mussolini to put a halt to further potentially hazardous voyages. As a result, the expedition that left for the Baltoro had only limited exploratory and scientific scope. The team, led by Aimone of Savoy, Duke of Spoleto, took the first photogrammetric measurements of the Baltoro, and reached the northern (Chinese) face of K2, a side which had only been reached previously by Younghusband. During the expedition, many passes, glaciers and peaks were named, and the first maps of the entire Baltoro region were produced. Among the team was a young geologist from Friuli called Ardito Desio, who had met the Duke in the Dodecannese, and was already well known for his research in Libya. Ardito Desio would never forget the experience, and put it to good use when, in 1953, he was nominated by the CAI as the leader of the Italian K2 expedition.

In the twenty-five year period that followed the Spoleto expedition, there were three attempts on the peak by teams from the USA. The first of these, in 1938, was organised by the American Alpine Club, and led by Dr Charles Houston. The Americans began their attempt on the Abruzzi Spur on 1 July, passing the highest point reached by the Italians twenty-nine years before, to arrive at a steep rock band. The most critical part of this face is a slanting cleft at 6,650 metres, now known as 'House's Chimney' in honour of Bill House who was the first to climb it. Charles Houston and Paul Petzoldt reached the 'Shoulder' at 7,800 metres: at this point the angle of the Abruzzi Spur lessened before steepening to the final pyramid. The pair bivouacked at this point, but they were forced to descend the next day as they had forgotten the matches to light the stove and so had been unable to cook or melt snow.

The following year another American expedition was organised by Fritz Wiessner, a German who had emigrated to the USA. On the afternoon of 19 July 1939, Wiessner and his climbing partner, the Sherpa Pasang Dawa Lama, reached a height of about 8,400 metres, only 200 metres from the summit. Wiessner was equipped with hobnail boots, a hemp rope and wooden ice axes. However it wasn't his clothing or rudimentary equipment that stopped the summit climb, but his climbing partner Pasang Dawa Lama. The Sherpa refused to continue because of his fear that nightfall would mean an encounter with a pantheon of Tibetan demons at the summit. 'The Sherpa was immovable' said Wiessner many years later. 'I was tempted to remove the rope and climb to the top on my own, but I have never abandoned a colleague'.

Wiessner returned to a lower camp with the intention of making another attempt later. However, bad weather and a series of fatalities forced him to abandon the attempt. During the descent, Dudley Wolfe died, as did the Sherpas Pasang Kitar, Pasang Kikuli and Phinsoo who had gone up the mountain to rescue him.

If Wiessner had reached the 8,611 metre summit that day in July 1939, the history of mountaineering would have taken a different course, but the first of the 8,000 metre peaks to be climbed was the easier, and lower, Annapurna, some eleven years later.

The years immediately after Wiessner's climb saw no further activity on K2: firstly there was the war, which inhibited all forms of mountaineering, and then there were the turbulent years of Indian Independence and the separation of Pakistan. Not until 1953 did another expedition set out for K2. It was led by Dr Charles Houston, fifteen years after his first attempt, this time leading a new group of seven, mainly American, climbers. They were stopped at the Shoulder by ten days of violent snowstorms. Having decided to abandon the attempt, one team member, Art Gilkey, who had been seriously weakened by a pulmonary oedema aggravated by the high altitude, was lost during the descent.

The American expedition was followed with trepidation by the Italians, who, in 1952, had suffered a 'diplomatic defeat' by the Americans in securing permission from Pakistan for a K2 expedition in 1953. The request for an attempt in 1954 was made by Ardito Desio on behalf of the CAI, assisted by the De Gasperi government through the usual diplomatic channels. The proposed expedition was discussed by the Central Council of CAI at a meeting in Parma on 24 April 1953 and again at Revolto on 24 May. Ardito Desio and the famous Lecco mountaineer Riccardo Cassin were nominated as the expedition leaders. At the Revolto meeting Desio announced that financing had been secured, via the National Research Council. On 27 July, the Prime Minister of Pakistan, Mohammed Ali, granted permission for an expedition to the Karakoram, to be led by Ardito Desio, on behalf of the CAI.

On 18 August Ardito Desio and Riccardo Cassin left on a reconnaissance mission. They travelled to Karachi and on 1 September met the members of the retreating American expedition. They then made their way to Skardu, and from there crossed the more than 70 kilometres of the Baltoro Glacier, reaching the American Base Camp at the foot of the Abruzzi Spur on 26 September 1953. They returned to Italy on 18 October. On 7 November the Central Council of CAI announced the names of the K2 executive committee. The record states that the leader of the expedition was to be Ardito Desio, with Riccardo Cassin as climbing leader. However, this collaboration came to nothing as Cassin was subsequently excluded from the expedition for health reasons.

Now in sole control, Ardito Desio began to attend to the organisational details. He travelled to Zurich, Vienna and London to look at the equipment that had been used on the Everest and Nanga Parbat expeditions, though most of the equipment that the climbers used was actually designed and manufactured by Italian companies, as it was intended that expedition serve as a shop window for Italian ingenuity. Most of the companies involved offered their equipment, much of it designed specifically for this expedition, free of charge. The final list of financial contributors to the expedition[*] consisted of hundreds of names, the number an indication of the national enthusiasm for the attempt. The CAI itself raised more than 4 million lire. A further 20 million lire were secured from Coni (Italian National Olympic Committee), and the long list of private and business donations guaranteed a sum in excess of 55 million lire. Adding another 10 million lire from the proceeds of the various publications, and 50 million lire from the government (requested in November 1953 and confirmed one year later through a special law relating to the National Research Council), the final total raised reached 140 million lire, corresponding today to about 1,735,000 euros (about £1.2 million or $2.1 million). Given the favourable exchange rate that existed with Pakistan at the time and the free supply of equipment, that was a very considerable sum.

One of the tasks Desio had was the choosing of the climbers for the expedition. A list of possible candidates was drawn up in Milan on 15 December 1953. Following two training and selection camps during the winter (16–27 January at Piccolo Cervino (Little Matterhorn) and 16–26 February at Monte Rosa), and a series of medical examinations and psychological tests, the final list was drawn up. The team was, listing the names in order of their homes, from east to west: Cirillo Floreanini from Friuli, Lino Lacedelli from Cortina d'Ampezzo, Gino Soldà from Vicenza, Erich Abram from Alto Adige, Walter Bonatti from Monza, Pino Gallotti from Milan, Achille Compagnoni from Valtellina, Ugo Angelino from Biella, and Ubaldo Rey, Sergio Viotto and Mario Puchoz from Val d'Aosta. Guido Pagani from Piacenza was chosen as the team's

---

[*] *Elenco dei sottoscrittori per la spedizione italiana*, Monthly Journal of the Italian Alpine Club, Turin, 1954, Vol. LXXIII, File 9-10.

doctor, and Mario Fantin, the film director and mountaineer from Bologna, was included to document the expedition. In addition, the cameraman Tom Hormann joined the expedition with the job of recording the first stages of the ascent so that he could return to Italy early and ensure the recordings were seen by the public on newsreels. There was also a scientific research group comprising Paolo Graziosi (ethnography), Francesco Lombardi (topography), Antonio Marussi (geophysics) and Bruno Zanettin (petrography).

Despite many difficulties with the delivery of the equipment, on 30 March 1954 the expedition equipment was loaded onto the steamship *Asia,* which belonged to Lloyd Triestino. The members of the mountaineering and scientific teams left separately, meeting up between Rawalpindi and Skardu at the end of April. On 30 April, Ardito Desio, Erich Abram, Mario Fantin and Tom Hormann made a reconnaissance flight around K2. On the same day the first group of porters began their march to the foot of the mountain. A total of 502 Balti porters* left Skardu, others joining along the way. The march in, which took until 29 May, was plagued by strikes, thefts and other problems.

Having set up Base Camp on 30 May, sixty-three of the porters were persuaded to transfer 1,500 kilograms of equipment and provisions to Camp I at 5,400 metres. On the same day, Lacedelli, Bonatti, Gallotti and Puchoz climbed the Abruzzi Spur and established Camp II, while Rey and Compagnoni carried out a reconnaissance climb to the proposed site of Camp III at 6,378 metres. The big climbing game had begun.

To assist with the transport of equipment and provisions up the first part of the Spur, which is a long snow slope, a 'cable lift' was constructed, comprising ropes and a winch, which, in three sections, reached 6,400 metres, just above Camp III. The first section was successfully tested on 2 June, and on 10 June, Compagnoni and Rey, who had been chosen as the advance rope party,

---

* The expedition used both Balti and Hunza porters. The Baltis are of Indo-Arian origin and live in the region of Baltistan in which the Baltoro Glacier and K2 are situated. The Baltis were employed as porters as far as Base Camp. To carry loads up the Abruzzi Spur the expedition used Hunza porters. Hunzas are of uncertain ethnic origin, and live in various high valleys of Pakistan. Although considered less capable than Nepalese Sherpas, the Hunzas are often employed as high altitude porters.

established Camp III. On 14 June the same pair established Camp IV at 6,560 metres. On 18 June the weather broke and, at about the same time, many of the climbers began to show signs of ill-health. Among them, at Camp II, was Mario Puchoz. At first his condition did not cause great concern, but on 20 June his condition worsened drastically, and on the next day he died in the arms of his distraught colleagues. The expedition doctor, Guido Pagani, diagnosed a form of galloping pneumonia. On 26 June the weather eased and Puchoz was carried to Base Camp: he was buried near a rocky spur at the junction of the Godwin-Austen and Savoy glaciers, where a memorial stone to those who have lost their lives on K2 stands.

Both stunned and spurred on by the death of their companion, the climbers resumed the work on the Spur. On 30 June, after successfully negotiating 'House's Chimney', Compagnoni and Rey set up Camp V at 6,678 metres. Then for two weeks severe blizzards swept the mountain, making the transporting of loads difficult, resulting in problems with the Hunza porters and a general deterioration in the health of the team. Compagnoni went down with severe earache, and, on 7 July, Floreanini fell 250 metres from just below Camp III, when a rope fixed by the Americans in 1953 broke. Floreanini miraculously survived, the fall resulting in no more than cuts and bruises. Finally, on 15 July, after overcoming a difficult rock section, Lacedelli and Bonatti established Camp VI at 6,970 metres.

During subsequent days these two, together with Compagnoni and Rey, carried loads and fixed ropes as far as Camp VII, despite very strong winds, bad weather and the fact that this was a particularly long and difficult section of the Spur, crossing a huge triangular wall of the 'Black Pyramid'. Exhausted by the technical difficulty of the climbing, and because of the poor weather, Lacedelli, Compagnoni and Rey descended to Base Camp on 22 July. After a short rest, they climbed up again, and on 25 July they reached Camp V. In their absence, Gallotti, Bonatti and Abram had pushed the route over the 'black rock' and had reached the Shoulder where they set Camp VII at 7,345 metres. Above there were different problems: though less steep, the climbing was through deep snow, that and the thin air making progress exhausting. On 28 July, Lacedelli, Compagnoni, Abram, Gallotti and Rey set off to establish Camp VIII, hoping to reach 7,630 metres. Rey had to return to Camp VII because he was exhausted, but the others all reached the proposed site. Abram and Gallotti returned to Camp VII the same evening, and the next day Gallotti and Bonatti reached Camp VIII with equipment and provisions. In the meantime, Lacedelli and Compagnoni set out towards the proposed site of the ninth and final camp. After a long, tiring climb, they decided to return to Camp VIII having left loads at the highest point they had reached.

And so we arrive at 30 July. On that day Lacedelli and Compagnoni retraced their path of the previous day, picked up the loads they had left and succeeded in climbing the ice wall that towered above Camp VIII. After negotiating rocks to the left they set up the small tent that became Camp IX, just above 8,000 metres, somewhat away from the direct climbing line. On the same day, Gallotti and Bonatti returned to Camp VII, and then climbed back up with Abram and the Hunza porters Mahdi and Isah-Khan. Isah-Khan stayed with Gallotti at Camp VIII while Bonatti continued climbing with Mahdi and Abram, carrying the oxygen cylinders required for the final assault on the summit. They continued climbing, although exhausted, in the knowledge that the oxygen would be vital for Lacedelli and Compagnoni, and for the success of the expedition. In the afternoon, however, Abram, overcome with exhaustion, also had to give up and returned to Camp VIII.

In the early evening, Bonatti and Mahdi finally succeeded in overcoming the last ice wall at nearly 8,000 metres, but were unable to locate the tent that had been pitched by Lacedelli and Compagnoni. When they finally saw it, it was too late to reach it, and the two of them were forced to prepare a dramatic bivouac, with no equipment, at 8,000 metres, with little chance of survival. Next morning, weak but still alive, Bonatti and Mahdi, who was showing signs of delirium, left the oxygen where it was and somehow managed to return to Camp VIII. Lacedelli and Compagnoni went down to pick up the oxygen where their companions had left it and were then ready for the final climb. They set off in deep snow, then moved left on to a rocky, ice-covered wall. Despite the difficulty and the fact that the oxygen had run out, just before 18.00 they reached the summit. At 8,611 metres, K2 is the second highest mountain on earth and probably the most difficult.

The time for celebration was, however, short. After taking a few photos and shooting a short cine-film it was necessary to descend. Compagnoni lost a glove and Lacedelli gave him one of his own. By now night had fallen and their only battery was just about useless. To add to the problems, both Lacedelli and Compagnoni were suffering from frostbite because of the extreme cold and high altitude. The going became much more difficult, some of the stretches of rock that they had climbed being completely impossible to descend. The descent became a long drawn out torment full of hidden dangers. At one point Compagnoni fell, but Lacedelli managed to hold him. Then both men fell into crevasses, fortunately full of snow, that had opened up below Camp IX. Exhausted, they lost their way, but finally, at 11pm, they reached Camp VIII. In the two days that followed, assisted by their colleagues, they reached Base Camp. The festivities were muted, however, because of the pain caused by their frostbitten fingers. This, together with the phlebitis that meant Gallotti could not walk, made the return journey very slow. Finally, having started out on 11 August, the team arrived at Skardu on the 23rd.

On 3 September Compagnoni, Rey, Fantin and Pagani returned to Italy by plane, while Desio remained in Pakistan to complete the scientific research, which had been an integral part of the expedition. On 10 September the remaining climbers left for Italy on the *Asia*. They disembarked at Genoa on 30 September where a cheering crowd, including Charles Houston, leader of the American 1953 expedition, was waiting. On 8 October Desio returned to Italy, though it was not until 12 October that the names of the two summit climbers were officially confirmed (though the press had already predicted that it had been Compagnoni and Lacedelli). The adventure was over.

On the steamship Asia, *returning to Italy after the successful climb of K2. From the bottom: Ugo Angelino, Walter Bonatti, Cirillo Floreanini, Pino Gallotti, Gino Soldà, Erich Abram, Lino Lacedelli and Sergio Viotto.*

Part 2

Lacedelli Talks

The following interview is distilled from many hours of recording, the transcripts being revised several times by Lacedelli during the summer and autumn of 2003. Though Lacedelli's memory is extraordinary, he can be excused the small number of memory lapses after fifty years. But most of the responses are both precise and detailed as Lacedelli was able to draw on the diaries he meticulously kept during the 1954 expedition, diaries which give dates and altitudes throughout the ascent.

The Choice

GIOVANNI CENACCHI: *How many other times have you told all the story in your own words?*

LINO LACEDELLI: I have told parts of the story on occasions, but never the whole story. There are many details ... details which I am now able to reveal. For example, the events of Camp IX – I have never told the whole story of what happened there. There are many other details that I have also never revealed.

The official report, the one signed by Compagnoni and yourself, did you write it together?
I didn't write it. They probably made me sign it, but I don't remember exactly. At the time, my major concern was avoiding involvement in the media controversy. That was why, sometimes, I confirmed things even when I knew they hadn't happened exactly like that.

The only version that I remember having been personally involved in was the interview that Compagnoni and myself gave in Milan to Dino Buzzati, which subsequently appeared in *Corriere della Sera*. Buzzati interviewed us, which I remember he did very well, and then sent the transcripts to Charles Houston in America. It was also published in *Life* magazine. I remember saying to Compagnoni before the interview: 'If you don't get it right, I'll give you a kick in the shins every time you make a mistake!'

Let's start at the beginning. How were you contacted, and then chosen for the expedition?
At Cortina we had known for some time that the Alpine Club was

organising an expedition to K2. So, Guido Lorenzi, Bibi Ghedina[*] and myself set about getting ourselves noticed in the mountaineering world. Attilio Tissi, the senator and mountaineer, came to Cortina one day and said: 'I need your resumé to send to Milan ... so that you can be considered'. Some 220 requests arrived in Milan from all the sections of CAI. A specially-created Committee chose twenty-two from these, including Bibi Ghedina and myself. Unfortunately Guido Lorenzi wasn't picked: he had hurt himself in a motor bike accident and they weren't able to include him. I was very sorry because I thought he had a good chance. Soon after, in December, Bibi Ghedina broke his leg. So that only left me, which was really sad.

Which of your previous climbs do you think brought you to the attention of the Committee?
In 1951, Bibi and myself had gone to the Gran Capucin where we made the first repeat of Bonatti's route in one day, without a bivouac. That climb in the Western Alps, for us coming from the Dolomites, was important in getting us noticed outside our own area. Also in 1951, we made our first attempt on the south-west face of the Scotoni. We completed the route the following summer. Then, to give us as much experience as possible in an environment similar to the Himalayas, in January 1952 I climbed the *Eötvos-Dimai* route on the south side of the Tofana di Rozes, with Albino Michielli and Guido Lorenzi. That was supposed to be a practice for a winter climb of the *Solleder* on the Civetta, but unfortunately I went down with bronchitis so that didn't happen.

What was your first contact with the expedition?
We went to Milan for a medical examination. I already knew Floreanini, Pagani, Abram and Bonatti and had climbed with some

---

[*] Guido Lorenzi and Luigi 'Bibi' Ghedina, who were also members of the Società Scoiattoli di Cortina d'Ampezzo (Squirrels' Club of Cortina), and Lino Lacedelli became well-known in 1952 when they completed a new route on the south-west wall of the Scotoni. The climb made a great impression in climbing circles, especially the overcoming of a key passage on the route when the three formed a human pyramid of three in *etriers*.

of them. I didn't know any of the others. I only knew Compagnoni by sight.

You had already climbed with Bonatti?
Yes, we had climbed the *Direttissima degli Scoiattoli* on the Grande of the Cinque Torri. In Milan, Professor Desio told us that he had organised a winter camp at the Piccolo Cervino in order to agree on equipment and provisions, but also so that we could get to know each other.

Eighteen of us went to Piccolo Cervino. Captain Peyronel,* who was from Val d'Aosta, was given the job of making the final choice. After a first selection we were reduced to sixteen or seventeen: the important thing was that I was still in the group. Then we went to Milan where Professor Desio explained the details of the expedi-tion to us, including all the difficulties we would have to face. There was a second camp at Monte Rosa in February at Colle del Lys where we had our tents. From there we climbed the *Cresta del Lyskamm*, continuing to the summit of Monte Rosa. It was a beau-tiful, gorgeous day...

On our return to Milan we were told who the final eleven would be and it included me. I considered myself to be very lucky. However, we were already late with preparations and permissions for the expedition, and in the autumn of 1953 Professor Desio and Riccardo Cassin went to inspect the area as far as Base Camp. While they were there they were told of a glacier that was moving towards one of the nearby villages.** The authorities had asked for Desio's expert geological opinion. He said: 'No, don't worry, the glacier will stop moving'. He then went to meet the returning,

---

* Ardito Desio gave Captain Enrico Peyronel, an official of the Military Alpine School at Aosta, the task of observing the climbers selected during the two camps organised during the winter of 1954 on the Plateau Rosa and Monte Rosa. Peyronel drew up a final classification on the basis of thirteen criteria.

** In just a few months, the Kutiah glacier in the Stak valley had extended by 12 kilo-metres, threatening a village. It was feared that the glacier might block the valley of the Indus. It is claimed by some that Desio's expert opinion, that the people were not in danger, helped sway the Pakistani government to grant permission to the Italians for the ascent of K2.

The K2 team in Milan in the winter of 1954. From the left: Bruno Zanettin (petrologist), Achille Compagnoni, Lino Lacedelli, Walter Bonatti, Mario Puchoz, Ubaldo Rey, Erich Abram, Ardito Desio, Pino Gallotti, Gino Soldà, Cirillo Floreanini, Ugo Angelino, Sergio Viotto, Guido Pagani, and Paolo Graziosi (ethnographer).

unsuccessful, American expedition. On his return, he was told that the glacier had indeed stopped moving, just as he had predicted.

There were many applications for K2 for the following year, from countries all over the world. It is possible that the advice about the glacier helped us to obtain the permission from the Pakistani government. Desio was always boasting that this was the case, but we didn't really believe him. I was also aware that De Gasperi himself had played an important role. In my opinion the intervention of De Gasperi was significant. I don't know what he had promised the Pakistanis to persuade them. All I know is that, when we arrived in Lahore we met an Italian company from Friuli that was involved in a building project. There was a crowd of Baltis, about a hundred of them, waiting with their traditional baskets. I remember those from the company complaining, saying that even if the Baltis were given a good kicking it was still impossible to get them to work. At Karachi we had dinner with some other

Italians who were managing another construction company. We also saw other Italian construction companies in Rawalpindi. There were a lot of Italians working out there.

It might not have been a coincidence. Perhaps the contracts and commercial agreements were worth more than the expert geological opinion of Ardito Desio in convincing the Pakistani government to grant permission to the Italians.

I believe so, yes. Anyway, when the permission came through we were very late with the preparations, especially with equipment. So we divided the responsibilities. Each of us was given a list of companies to contact. To get everything ready we worked for a month and a half in Milan. My job was to take care of the propane gas cylinders. A large part of the work was packing them away in the boxes. Each box had to weigh exactly twenty-seven and a half kilograms. The problem was that there was always something missing and not all the companies were able to send the equipment in time.

But the preparations were eventually completed and the date of departure fixed. I went home for a few days to rest, then on 18 April I said goodbye to a few people: my aunt and uncle, my siblings and my fiancée, and then went to Milan. The first person I met there was Abram, at the Sempione Hotel. Then the others arrived and there was a big party. It was good to see everyone again after the camps. We were all very happy to have been chosen.

Regarding the selection, did you get the impression that there was any discrimination in the group, or that climbers from the Dolomites were considered less well adapted to the conditions you would meet on K2 than those from the Western Alps?

Well, it was a common prejudice, the same old suspicion. However, I must say that Peyronel was always very impartial and correct. He saw that we did as we were told, and he tried to be friendly with everyone. He was rather surprised by those of us from the Dolomites: occasionally he said that we were more open than his 'own' people. He was very complimentary about us, especially when we were setting up the camps. During the selection

meetings the camp sites were always in the most difficult positions
to get us used to the conditions we could expect. It was a great surprise to Peyronel to discover that those of us from the Dolomites
were easily able to deal with ice and mixed conditions.

Were there also climbing tests?
Yes, there was one occasion on a training rock. There was always
this friendly rivalry between the Westerners and ourselves. One
day Gallotti, Floreanini, Abram and myself were at Cervinia, at the
bottom of the training rock where we were to do the test. The test
involved climbing a dihedral already fitted with pitons. When we
reached the dihedral we decided we would play a trick. So we carried on, myself in the rear, pulling out the pitons. The next day,
Compagnoni and Desio brought us along, and explained the test.
He showed us the dihedral and we pretended to see it for the first
time. We climbed it without ropes and I climbed down, again without ropes. Then we confessed everything and we asked if they
wanted us to put the pitons back in. Desio was not pleased and
went away very annoyed. Anyway, at least we had demonstrated
that we were also able to climb on granite.

*Did you have the impression that Desio preferred those from Val d'Aosta
to yourselves?*
Yes, though more than anything Desio preferred those who agreed
with him. Most of us were not happy with this. We were not the
sort of characters to flatter the expedition leader. We did what we
had to do and that was all.

Who did the most flattering?
Most of all it was Compagnoni. He flattered Desio and vice versa.
This annoyed us a lot, particularly later on when Desio made him
leader of the first climbing group. None of us felt he deserved this.
In the second group Soldà was nominated as leader. I was in the
second group. I remember wondering to myself whether this
meant that we were worth less than the Hunza or Balti porters. But
we didn't take it too seriously. During a discussion with Floreanini
and some of the others I remember saying: 'We certainly haven't
come here to sunbathe, let's try and achieve what we can'.

Do you think that Riccardo Cassin's[*] exclusion from the expedition was as a result of him being too well respected as a mountaineer?
Desio's version was that Cassin was unable to take part for health reasons. Varicose veins were mentioned, amongst other things. But that wasn't the real reason. If Cassin had come, all the newspapers would have focused on him rather than Desio. To me that was obvious. Cassin never got over it. He's still upset today. For us climbers, having Cassin along would have been really great. We knew him well, we got on with him well, and he would have been much easier to talk to about the daily problems we faced during the climb.

It is said that the regime was too militaristic for a group of mountaineers used to operating more freely.
Every morning, Desio would write down the orders of the day along with Compagnoni. Then Compagnoni would come outside and attach them to the tent. We were expected to follow them without further discussion. The first time it happened we were surprised … afterwards we were annoyed.

Then there was the problem with the Hunza porters. Many of them did as little as they could get away with. They were always complaining about being ill, and never wanted to go on. Occasionally it was necessary to take one or two aside and show them the ice axe. When we told Desio about this he got angry, saying that we should treat them better. It's easy to make such judgements, but you needed to be there to see for yourself. He was always telling us off for treating the porters badly. However, this didn't stop him from ordering Angelino to leave half of the porters' sunglasses behind, because, according to him they didn't need them.

---

[*] Riccardo Cassin, a very strong alpinist, famous for several sixth grade routes in the 1930s, was proposed by CAI as the expedition's climbing leader. That would have meant his taking over from Desio in directing operations above Base Camp. After Desio's opposition, and thanks to a medical diagnosis, one which provoked many arguments, the CAI's Executive Committee for K2 excluded him from the expedition, alleging reasons of health, and the impossibility, considering his physical condition, of finding him an insurance policy. After 1954 Cassin began an intense programme of climbing around the world: he didn't give up walking in the mountains until he was 95.

Did you ever try talking to Desio, or complaining?
It wasn't possible to discuss anything with Desio. We weren't happy with the issue of the daily orders, but during the walk-in we didn't make too much fuss about it. I remember him writing one which said: 'If anyone doesn't obey my orders they will be punished with the most powerful weapon in the world, the press!' I remember Angelino tearing down that particular note and putting it in his pocket, saying: 'We'll take this to Milan'. I think we understood then that there was no chance of any discussion with Desio. In the high camps, when we were on the Spur, we would leave messages for sending down to the Professor. But he never took any notice of our requests. At one point we decided that we couldn't carry on like that anymore. But we had come all this way to climb the mountain and hopefully to get to the summit, so we talked to Dr Pagani, who was more approachable, because we knew we couldn't talk to Desio. But nothing changed: Desio carried on giving his daily orders, but for us it was like he didn't exist. His orders were no good, they didn't help us with our problems. All we wanted was for him to listen to us for a change, all of us, together. We wanted to be able to discuss our problems with him to see if he could come up with any ideas. Obviously we accepted that he was the leader of the expedition, but he should have come up with ideas to help us, not just issue orders. But it never happened.

He was very good at telling us off, even when we were exhausted. He was always saying: 'No, we must keep going!' He was a real military type, which irritated us greatly. Up at high altitude it isn't like it is lower down, nerves are easily frayed. I remember on one occasion, Dr Pagani wanted to come with us. 'No, you are staying here doctor!' said Desio. Pagani replied: 'I'm going with them because that's my job. I'm not staying here with nothing to do!'

How did the chain of command work?
Desio made all the decisions from Base Camp. He decided who would go up and what their objectives were. For a while we played this game, then we started to respond only to the requests for equipment, porters and climbers, which came down from the most advanced rope party on the Spur. We always responded to

the requests from those in the highest camp because they had the best idea of what was needed. Naturally Desio would get upset because he wanted to be in control and to direct the climbers according to his wishes.

Paying the porters at Urdukas.

Towards K2

After the preparation work you finally arrived in the Karakoram. What were your first impressions of these mountains, which were so different from those you were used to?

It was hard at first. I came down with a terrible bout of dysentery. The first group left on 30 April. The next day it was supposed to be my turn. I remember Pagani coming to me and saying; 'We need to send you home'. 'No', I replied, 'Over my dead body!' The next day they asked me how I was feeling and I said I was fine, though in actual fact I could hardly stand up. I said to the others: 'I'll be right behind you. If I fall over when you stop, please put me back on my feet.' I remember very little about that first stage. I was too ill. Anyway, it was interesting to see all those peaks of over 6,000 metres with extraordinary faces that reminded me of the Dolomites: there was even one which resembles the Campanile Basso.

The Trango Towers?

Wonderful, fantastic! I don't remember them very well, but I recall there were faces more than 1,000 metres high. Beautiful! I also remember all the people who came out to look at us. Particularly the children. We would give them coloured paper from the boxes and they would get really excited because they had never seen it before. We also gave then empty jam tins. We would turn over the edges so that they wouldn't cut their lips and tell them they could be used for drinking *pani*, water. Further on, at Askole, the last village, we stopped for a rest day. One group of porters had already gone on ahead: we were with the second group. The weather had been bad and when we arrived on the Baltoro Glacier the going

Crossing the Biaho river.

was very tiring because of black ice covered with stones which moved. We had to be very careful not to end up head over heels.

On the glacier none of the porters, not even the ones who knew the way, wanted to lead the way, so we had to go ahead to find a route. The porters were just too lazy and spent all the time moaning. There were some good ones of course. There were some young boys, one of whom was really great. We called him *Birichin* (Little Scamp). He was sixteen years old and very willing. He was always helpful and he wanted to learn Italian. We chose the best ones to carry our personal equipment, and in the end the better ones helped us a lot.

In general, though, it wasn't easy. Every evening there were problems getting the porters to go to sleep. We had to round them up like sheep, take hold of one or two and throw them under the tarpaulins. We used to make a type of tent, hanging the tarpaulins around the cases. Unfortunately they were not very keen on staying inside, preferring to be out in the open. They would use bare rock as a base, then put down some bags made from animal skins.

Then they would take off all their clothes and lie down, two or three of them. Then they would cover themselves with more bags and go to sleep like that. I remember one night we had 20 centimetres of snow. They just carried on snoring without moving. They were sleeping naked with 20 centimetres of snow on top of them. I suppose they were used to it.

Going to bed was always a complicated business, and we always got to our tents late, at half past ten or eleven o'clock, completely exhausted. One evening I remember taking off my trousers, putting them under my head and turning over. Then I felt a hand trying to take them away. It was one of the Baltis. It would have been a problem if they had stolen my trousers, finding another pair amongst all the other stuff would have been difficult.

There were also other problems during the walk-in. Many of the porters were barefoot and the doctor was kept busy because they were always cutting their feet. We also helped out. But the problem was that they got used to going to the doctor every day, either with a stomach-ache or a headache. Pagani would say: 'We can't give

Mario Fantin on a precarious temporary bridge during the walk-in.

medicine to everyone otherwise we won't have any left'. So we decided to give them *Lifesavers,* the energy-giving coloured sweets with holes in them. We thought: 'We'll give them one colour for stomach-ache, and another colour for headache'. Pagani would say: 'Take this with water'. After a while they were all better!

The first major problem with the porters was at Urdukas, at 4,000 metres. A group of them had gone on ahead with Desio, others were with us. Then we saw them turn back, holding each other by the hands. They had been snow-blinded because they didn't have sunglasses, which are indispensable at that height. But some of them had sunglasses – they were still in their pockets. There was pandemonium. Desio blamed Angelino, accusing him of having left the sunglasses behind. He said: 'Tomorrow, you're going home'. But we knew what had really happened: it had been Desio himself who had given the order to leave half of the sunglasses behind at Skardu because he thought we had enough. I remember Angelino coming out saying: 'So you're going to send me home are you?!' One after the other we all went to Desio and said: 'We're going home too ...'. And that's how it finished.[*]

After the incident there was a lot to do. The porters who had been blinded needed eyewashes, but in the end we had to send many of them home because they couldn't see. Then we had to give our spare glasses, even our personal ones, to those porters who didn't have them.

Was that the only crisis on the journey to the mountain?
No, when we reached Concordia we realised that we were out of flour. The Baltis had opened our cases and taken the flour and biscuits. At Urdukas there was a warehouse full of flour and so we decided to go back with about thirty porters. We left early in the morning and we arrived after two days: it had snowed at Urdukas and we sank in the soft snow – we were exhausted as we had to create the track entirely ourselves because the Baltis refused to

---

[*] This episode was confirmed by Ugo Angelino in his letter to the CAI Executive Committee for K2 on 29 December 1954. The letter was published in the *Monthly Journal of the Italian Alpine Club* (Vol. LXXIV, File 9-10, Turin 1955), and was also in Fulvio Campiotti's book, *K2* (Eli, Milan, 1954).

Porters pass the Towers of Biacedi during the walk-in.

help. At Urdukas we found Sadiq, who was in charge of the porters, and he immediately gave us something to eat and drink. We asked him to send chapatis as soon as possible, because the situation at the Concordia camp had become very difficult: the porters only ate flour and apricots, and the flour had run out completely. Fortunately the weather improved, though it was very cold. I remember leaving early next morning, at that time it was still snowing hard. We were able to reach camp that evening and to announce that the flour would be arriving the next morning. And it did.

That was a close shave, and you were only one day's journey from Base Camp.
Yes, the day we left for Base Camp was a beautiful day. After four hours walking we finally saw K2 in all its glory.

When we arrived we started to pitch the tents, for ourselves and for cooking. But the problems with the porters were not over. Because of the delay over the flour we were behind schedule. At Urdukas we had had to resort to threats because some of the porters had wanted to boycott the expedition. There was nearly a riot – and there were a lot of them and not many of us. There was a lot of arguing – one minute they wanted to go back, the next they didn't, but wouldn't go on. It was frustrating as we just wanted to, and still needed to, move provisions and equipment. At Base Camp the problems surfaced again, but with the help of Sadiq and Colonel Ata Ullah,* we managed to convince sixty-three porters to carry loads as far as the base of the Spur, at 5,400 metres. But some of them didn't want to go on, in spite of the *bakshish* and the cigarettes. So we increased the bribes and eventually got going, setting flags along the first part of the climb to mark the route because of the danger of crevasses. Along the way there were more protests, which needed more rupees and cigarettes to sort out. Finally, with God's help, we arrived with all the equipment at 5,400 metres.

---

* Colonel Ata Ullah, who had already been involved with the American expedition of 1953, was sent by the Pakistani government as an observer. With him was a small group of officials who provided an escort throughout the expedition.

Above: Erich Abram helps a porter affected by snow blindness.

Below: Bonatti watches as Lacedelli, Floreanini and Viotto enjoy the hot springs at Chongo.

So Ata Ullah, the Pakistani Government's representative, proved to be a useful presence?
Yes, Ata Ullah had some power over the porters, though there was a problem as he wasn't able to speak the local dialects. Sadiq, the chief of the porters, was the only one who could. Sadiq was really on the ball. He could speak English and four or five local dialects. He was the one who kept the porters together. It was a stroke of luck having him along. I heard that later he became an engineer. Apart from those two there were three 'captains', but they weren't of much use. They just hung around, they would finish off the tea or the hot chocolate that was left over after breakfast. Sometimes they would finish off an entire saucepan: they were as greedy as children.

At Base Camp did you join up with the others?
The first to arrive at Base Camp were Rey, Compagnoni and Puchoz. Compagnoni and Rey had already gone ahead on a reconnaissance. The Americans had pitched their first camp in a completely different position to the one we had planned. I also went up to have a look. I remember saying: 'This is no good'. The place Compagnoni preferred was not a good choice for a camp, there was too big a risk of falling ice and avalanches. Back at Base Camp Desio showed us what the Americans had done: we had acquired a copy of their report that had been translated into Italian. While we were up there we had come to a conclusion about the best site, but, as usual, Desio told us what we had to do. In the end we decided to put the second camp at 6,000 metres, higher than the American one. The position was reasonably good: there were five tents, three for us and two for the Hunzas. That was at the beginning of June.

Camp II was pretty much an advanced Base Camp. It was the reference point for the loads. At Base Camp we had installed a sort of cable lift, 300 metres long, with a kind of sledge, which we set up in an area just above Camp I. With this we were able to transport a lot of equipment, in the end at least fifty loads of 25 to 30

Lino Lacedelli and Walter Bonatti on the Baltoro Glacier, May 1954.

Mitre Peak from Concordia.

kilos. The sledge worked well, except in bad weather. With fresh snow even two people couldn't move it.

Had the sledge been planned or was it improvised?
It was planned beforehand, because of the experience we had had with the porters. The Hunzas wouldn't carry heavy loads, no more than 10 kilos and generally around 5. And then they were a disaster in the tents. Some of them we sent home because they only seemed to be there to eat and make a mess. It was a constant battle. Fortunately we had Ata Ullah on our side. Desio, of course, was always against us. We were always having to offer more rupees. There were arguments every day.

Were the duties of the climbing groups well defined?
Floreanini and myself were in the second group. We were in charge of the supply lines so it was our responsibility to get the loads transported. In the first phase of the climb I was mostly worked with the cable lift. I was happy to do that, but a part of me

Lino Lacedelli in front of K2 after his return from the summit.

was miffed. I would say to myself: 'OK, if I have to be a mule I'll do it, but then we'll see'. Occasionally I would leave the sledge, and, from Camp II, I would carry a good load myself up to Camp IV. Sometimes 20 kilos or more. I was annoyed that the others were climbing higher and higher, and we had to stay down below acting as mules. At least when I was carrying the loads myself I was doing some climbing. I did a number of trips like that, and in the end it was useful for acclimatisation and fitness, though it was very hard work. We were actually the real porters, not the Hunzas! With them you agreed one thing and then you didn't see them again. You would go back down and discover they were still in the tent sleeping. It would drive you mad. We would send letters of complaint to Desio, but he would just tell us off. There were only a handful of porters that we could count on: Isah-Khan, Mahdi, Aminullah, Hidayat-Sha and Hidayat-Khan were the ones we depended on, and we tried to help them out with a bit of extra money. But we had to deal with them one at a time. That way we actually succeeded in taking two of them as far as Camp VIII.

When you were climbing the Spur, how free were you to make your own decisions?

Desio gave his orders by radio, based on what Compagnoni told him and then Compagnoni told us. For a while we played along, but then we told Compagnoni it wouldn't work. We said that the orders had to be based on the needs of those on the highest rope party. 'It should be the highest rope party in command, they know best what they need,' we said, 'not Desio, not even you'. 'I'm sorry,' Compagnoni would say, 'but Desio has spoken'. 'We couldn't care less', I said eventually, 'I will only respond to what Abram, Bonatti and the others tell me: if they tell me to carry up these things then we will carry up these things'. After that, above the first camps, we always worked like that, according to what those up higher wanted. Sometimes it was Compagnoni and Rey, sometimes Abram and Bonatti, and then there was Floreanini and myself.

I also took on the role of setting up the fixed ropes. I had already done some lower down with Gallotti, and others with Bonatti. The ones I did with Bonatti were the most difficult, in the mist, above Camp V and Camp VI. It was the most difficult stretch, on the Black Pyramid. We did them all and I remember working from five in the morning until five in the evening. But we were happy because at least we were higher up and closer to those in the first group. The idea of setting up fixed ropes, making travel between the camps easier, was a plan we agreed with Desio for a good reason. In case of illness or particularly bad weather, it was much easier to climb down to the camp below, even on your own. This turned out to be useful on many occasions.

Then it was 21 June....

The Sacrifice

21 June was the date of Mario Puchoz's death …
Yes, on the 18th, Puchoz wasn't feeling very well, but it didn't seem to be anything serious. Anyway Dr Pagani went up to check. We left together from Camp I, Floreanini was also there. He and I carried up some heavy loads, as well as some bedding. Pagani himself carried a Super K2 tent. The weather was awful, we couldn't see our tracks in the snow and large blocks of snow and ice showered down from above. We met Gallotti and Bonatti coming down in the snowstorm. They also weren't well, they both had sore throats. At Camp II we found Puchoz. He was pale and feeling very low. Then Compagnoni and Rey arrived, coming down from Camp IV to Base Camp: they weren't well either. Finally Abram, Viotto and Soldà arrived from above, having abandoned their packs just below Camp IV because of the blizzard. So Floreanini and myself had to go down because there was no more space.

Wouldn't it have been wiser to take Puchoz with you?
At the time his condition didn't seem so serious. Nothing out of the ordinary. Many of us were unwell. Anyway we asked him, but he didn't want to go down. He didn't want to return to Base Camp. 'I don't get on very well with Desio', he said, 'I would prefer to stay here'. We said our goodbyes and left for Camp I.

The next day we worked really hard. I went up on my own to the intermediate sledge station. Badur, the Hunza, followed, in his usual sedate way. I enlarged the area for the equipment by packing down the snow and we started sending loads up. By evening we

26 June, a very sad day. Mario Puchoz was buried at the foot of K2.

had pulled up twelve loads. All the time there was a really strong wind and it was snowing. While we were working a small dark thing struck me. I stopped it. It was one of Abram's gloves that had fallen all the way from Camp IV. On the 20th I carried on the hard work with Floreanini and Badur. Gallotti and Abram came down from Camp II to take up more loads. During the day Floreanini sent me a note to tell Dr Pagani that Bonatti was feeling unwell. But Pagani didn't come down, a sure sign that Puchoz was not recovering. While I was going down, I bumped into Viotto and Soldà searching for something among the equipment bags. Then Soldà set off towards Camp I. He told us he was taking up medicine for Dr Pagani because Puchoz was not well at all.

That morning, the weather was terrible. The wind was so strong, it was impossible to work. We wondered how Mario was. Floreanini started cooking and Bonatti decided to go back down because he wasn't feeling well. Then, while we were in the tent, we heard the sound of falling stones and knew that someone was coming down from Camp II. We thought that they might be trying to carry Puchoz down to Base Camp so that he could recover better. At 11.30, Floreanini went out of the tent and met Viotto. I heard him asking questions and then Viotto crying as he answered. Pagani arrived and I heard Angelino asking for news and the doctor replying that Mario had died during the night, without regaining consciousness. I only remember going to the doctor saying, 'No, no it's not possible, there must be a mistake, Mario only had a cough'. Pagani replied that, with that weather, at 6,000 metres, even a cough can be fatal.

Was it pneumonia or a high altitude pulmonary oedema?
I'm not sure, but Dr Pagani spoke about galloping bronchopneumonia. Everyone went down from Camp I: we were all feeling terrible, everyone with their own thoughts. I thought of Mario, who had worked hard alongside the rest of us, without complaining, during that horrible weather. It was like losing a brother. That's how we felt after all the dangers we had faced together. I remember thinking that we now had a mission to conquer the mountain that had killed our friend. We descended to Base Camp in silence. We wondered how to let his family know. Communication was a

Camp II.

problem up there. Suppose the newspapers got the name wrong: we were also worried about our own families.

Collecting Mario's body wasn't easy. The weather was terrible during the next few days. On the 25th Soldà, Viotto and myself went up together with three Hunzas. The mountain was covered with fresh snow and during the climb there were three huge avalanches: we saved ourselves only by jumping into a crevasse, the snow passing over our heads for a quarter of an hour. We arrived at Camp I where, luckily, the tents were all in one piece. The next day I went up with Viotto and the Hunza Mahdi, who was carrying a body bag. Camp II was buried in snow and poor Mario was in front of the tent. The descent was dangerous and very tiring, what with the threat of avalanches and everything. Lower down the others came to help. One thing I'll never forget was that when we arrived at the intermediate station we found two Hunzas praying. That was very moving. At five in the afternoon we finally arrived at Base Camp. No one was talking.

Next day we took Mario's body to a place nearby where there is a stone pyramid in memory of those who had lost their lives on K2: Gilkey, the Pasang brothers, Phinsoo and the others.*

It must have been difficult to start climbing again …
When we returned to the camp after burying Puchoz, Desio immediately said, 'Tomorrow you need to go back up!' That started a big argument because we wanted to be left alone for at least a day, after all we had lost one of our colleagues. But Desio was immovable. He wanted us to leave the next day. We went away very upset, but we did rest for one day as we had decided. And then we left, all of us thinking that we must get to the summit for Mario.

But our problems weren't over. A few days later, on 6 July, I was climbing above Camp III with Floreanini, towards the place where we had decided to set up the cable lift. The cable needed to go down to Camp II. We finished our work and began to go back down. At one point there was a 15 metre rock face. Floreanini went ahead, holding on to an old rope that had been left by the Americans. Suddenly the rope broke. I saw him fall about 7 metres, then another 10, and then he was sliding downwards through the snow, head first. He was like a ball, sliding along a ridge with a couloir on each side. 'It's over' I thought. It was like he was doing a slalom between lots of rocks sticking up through the snow. Behind me was the Hunza Aminullah, rigid with fear. I decided to go down after Floreanini, at first holding on to the ropes, then down a 65° slope. Floreanini continued to roll downwards for another 200 metres or so and came to rest on a piece of level ground: a true miracle.

When I reached him he was covered in blood, but he recognised me. I remember thinking, 'Poor Cirillo, so many broken bones.' Then I felt his legs, arms, back and head. Everything seemed to be OK. So I put my arms under his armpits and pulled him to his feet. I told him to try and support himself, and he could. That was a sure sign that nothing was broken, although he did have a bad headache. When Pagani and Angelino came to meet us at Camp II they looked terrified. They were so worried that they couldn't

* Victims of previous K2 expeditions. Their bodies were never found.

speak. 'He's OK, he's OK, we're coming', I shouted, trying to reassure them. Pagani gave Floreanini some *Simpathol*, and eventually we arrived at Camp II. The doctor gave him a good check-up. He had a cut on his head, one on his backside and another on his nose. He was covered in bruises, but there was nothing broken. Inside the tent Floreanini was chattering away because of the shock. He was saying that he had always liked me, which moved me. What a fall it had been, good grief! A terrible experience.

We began to feel that everything was against us. The weather was horrible, and it was only by chance that we hadn't lost another one of us. But luckily Floreanini was okay. We wanted to take him down to Base Camp, but he refused to go. He didn't want to see Desio either.

How come no-one wanted to go down to Desio?
No-one really liked him. Some time later, Desio and Ata Ullah came up to Camp II. We all disappeared. Only Floreanini was left, but Desio didn't go into his tent, not even to ask how he was feeling. I remember Floreanini shaking with anger saying, 'He didn't even say hello'. In my opinion that wasn't very nice. A leader should at least show some interest. He had heard about the accident hadn't he? It wouldn't have hurt him just to say hello, to say, 'You were lucky', or something like that. Possibly that experience strengthened Floreanini. He took a long time to get himself up and about, then he managed to climb to 7,400 metres, to Camp VII. Then he gave up. He was finished, but before his fall he had made big contributions, both high up and low down, and around the camps.

From your account it seems that, during the ascent, there was a kind of silent mutiny. Apart from the differences you had with Desio, did you have a certain amount of autonomy regarding decision making?
Well, when we went down we always tried to talk about any problems we had. But Desio would always say, 'Oh, that's nothing, it's not difficult, you must press on'. It's all very well to urge people on, but sometimes you also have to listen, and to try and understand people. All he would say was, 'No you must go on, it's not a big problem'. He would call us 'his little boys'. But it seemed that

he wasn't interested in how much effort and how many risks we had taken up there. It was an attitude which was bound to annoy us in the end. Since we would only argue, we ended up by talking to him as little as possible. It was inevitable. When we went down to Base Camp we were in need of a bit of rest. Fortunately Dr Pagani was there as well. When he saw that we were really annoyed by something Desio had said or done, he would try and make light of the situation. He would pull our legs, and tell us not to get so annoyed over such little things. We would end up laughing. That was the right attitude, the best way of treating us. At least he understood our problems. In the high camps, day to day life was difficult. At night it was difficult to sleep, and even something as simple as making soup was complicated. You had to melt the snow and cook in a restricted space. I used to eat *speck* (smoked ham) more than anything else, and that helped me. Often we were too tired to prepare anything to eat, not even soup. Sometimes bad weather would set in, and we would be marooned for days closed up in a tent. When we finally went out again we could hardly walk, just like after a long illness.

Reading Mario Fantin's diary, it seems that it was he, out of the whole group, who had the most problems with Ardito Desio….
At Skardu everyone organised a sleeping partner. Floreanini and Pagani, they had been friends for a long time, Rey and Compagnoni. In the end there was Puchoz, Fantin and myself. Puchoz decided he would stay on his own so I ended up with Fantin. He didn't have much to do. He was always at Base Camp, taking a bit of film here and there. He suffered because of this. He couldn't go up to take films because Desio didn't want him to, and he wouldn't let us help him. However, to help him we would secretly take up his tripod for him on occasion. Fantin was a mountaineer and could have gone past Camp IV, but Desio wouldn't let him. According to Desio, we should have been carrying loads up the mountain, not helping Fantin. But I think the film was important as well. Fantin was a good cinematographer. While he was taking a film at Camp II there was a blizzard, but he continued shooting and the same thing happened further up at Camp IV. I wish we had been able to help him climb up to Camp V or VI so

that he could have taken some film of the more difficult bits, up on the rocks. Up there, there is a key section called 'House's Chimney', with some grade 3 difficulties, and the Black Pyramid. While we were climbing there we managed to take a few bits of film ourselves, particularly Abram, but obviously not enough. Fantin would have been worth his weight in gold up there, but Desio would never let him go up that far, and that was a great shame. Fantin was very angry about it.

Was there tension within the climbing group or were you all united?
Not always. Everyone in the group had specific responsibilities. I remember I was supposed to check where all the tents were. I had to be sure they were all there. I was always counting them, and there was always one missing. The others were always pulling my leg, saying that I couldn't count. One day I mentioned to Pagani that there always seemed to be one tent missing. He said, 'I know why there's one less'. While we were away on the Spur he had had a look in our tents. In mine he found all the medicine he had given me. I would take it from him, but never actually swallow it! In Compagnoni's tent he found the missing tent, still in its packet. Then there was a big row.

Compagnoni tried to justify himself saying that he was saving it for his children. A tent, can you believe it? It was supposed to be used in the camps, on the Spur! So we had an argument. Compagnoni was given a hard time by everyone, even Pagani was really annoyed. If someone else had done something like that Desio would have sent him home. But Compagnoni was Desio's favourite. If it had happened at the end of the expedition it wouldn't have been so bad. I asked to keep my trousers and jacket at the end. I said that I was willing to pay for them, but they gave them to me. However, the point is, I asked.

Were there any other disagreements?
Yes, a few, but generally we tried to resolve problems between ourselves by talking, by helping each other. There was a minor matter with Soldà, who was unhappy at being appointed leader of the second group instead of the first. I remember being in one of the tents at Camp II and he was really furious. He was shouting, 'Why

has Desio put Compagnoni in charge? I should have been the leader because I've done much more climbing. And as for Angelino, why's he second in command? He's never achieved anything in climbing'. I said that at least Angelino was good at keeping accounts, and then I said, 'I don't know if you're so good … why are you telling me these things, go and tell Desio. Stop criticising. Be satisfied with what you've got'.

Since he had a lot of mountaineering experience he thought that he should have been the leader, but I don't think he would have been capable because he was too impulsive. He was also like that in the Dolomites. He would set off at a terrific pace and then grind to a halt. We would always be telling him to slow down. One day we had gone down from Camp IV to Camp II. Soldà was there with Bonatti. There was a blizzard and we were shut up in the tent. Then Soldà said that he was going outside for a moment. After a while, when he hadn't returned, Bonatti and I began to look for him in the blizzard. I was searching above the tent when I

Lacedelli operating the cable lift which aided load hauling between Camps II and III.

suddenly heard a strange noise. Eventually, I found him stuck in a chimney where he was throwing up. He was ill for three days and to this day I still don't understand where he wanted to go. He was like that. Occasionally his head made him do reckless things.

Generally though we all became good friends. There was a lot of teasing and leg pulling. We spent many happy days together even when the weather was bad. Each of us would tell stories of our adventures, and not only those on the mountains! Abram for example had a long list of female conquests. One of our prime targets for fun was Floreanini. When the post arrived we would often open his letters without him knowing. Poor Floreanini, we played so many tricks on him!

One day, at Camp IV, Gallotti was supposed to do the cooking. The only problem was that he was only just about able to make tea. On that occasion he was supposed to make a risotto using a pressure cooker. We were there pulling his leg as usual. In the end Abram, from outside the tent, advised him to open the lid of the pressure cooker. Obviously the rice exploded everywhere. I remember the tent was open and Rey was near the opening, without his boots. He threw himself outside onto the ground, rolling over and over, eventually coming to rest on top of a lower tent. We had to throw him a rope to rescue him. We rescued all the rice too!

House's Chimney.

The Summit

The weather started to improve some ten days before the final ascent. I assume you all started to make plans for the summit. What were Desio's orders regarding the attempt?

At Camp IV, during our descent to Base Camp on 22 July Rey, Compagnoni, Pagani and myself spoke about this. Pagani reminded us that someone would need to carry up the oxygen bottles. 'I'll take them up', I said, 'But I won't be coming back down'. So then we made our plan for taking up the bottles. The leading rope party was to be Compagnoni and Rey, and I was to be the support, with Abram I think.

Anyway we, that is Compagnoni, Rey and myself, went down to Base Camp that day. We had been up at high altitude for a long time and we needed to recuperate a little. At Base Camp we learned that Desio had also nominated Compagnoni and Rey as the lead rope party. As usual with Desio there were arguments. To him everything was black and white. In my opinion he didn't understand very much about mountaineering. He thought everything was simple and never took account of the real difficulties when he made his plans. He never understood the struggle that was taking place high on the mountain. I was so angry about so many things ... and then I felt I was really fit, well prepared. One day I had made two trips from Camp II to Camp IV carrying heavy loads. That was really good training. Anyway, around 23 July two New Zealanders from the United Nations told us by radio from Skardu that the forecast was for five or six days of good weather. The 24th was a beautiful day and so we set off from Base Camp, at 4,950 metres, loaded up with equipment. On the 26th I arrived at Camp VII, at 7,400 metres. It was beautiful there, with a nice level area for the tents and a marvellous view. Gallotti, Abram, Bonatti, Floreanini, Rey and Compagnoni all arrived. Soldà had had to retire somewhere between the Camps VI and VII. Floreanini had gone down with three Hunzas because there were no more places in the tents. Rey had got really tired out and wasn't feeling well. Gallotti and Bonatti also weren't well. The next day the weather was bad so we rested.

Was it useful?
On the 28th, Bonatti was out of action and Rey wasn't very well. There were five of us left: Gallotti, Abram, Compagnoni, Rey and myself. After only 100 metres climbing Rey couldn't go on, two of us actually had to help him back to the tent because he could hardly stand up. I remember him crying with frustration: he was supposed to be going to the summit, and he at least wanted to help us get there. The problem was that we had done no acclimatisation above 7,400 metres: we were concerned about it because as well as the ones who were already unwell, Gallotti was also doubtful. 'What are we going to do?' I asked, 'We haven't done any acclimatisation above this height'. I suggested we should continue, with me climbing with Abram, but he disagreed and suggested that I should go with Compagnoni. 'I'll come up later,' he said. 'If Gallotti recovers, we'll bring up the bags and sleeping mats'. And that's what they did. Compagnoni and I went up. Gallotti and Abram followed. The idea was to set up the next camp above the wall we could see, but when we got close to it we realised we would have to set camp below it, under a crevasse.

Was that Camp VIII?
Yes. In the afternoon we saw two dots in the distance. One was Gallotti, the beanpole. He would go forward three steps and then fall over, but when he finally arrived he was really pleased with himself. The same day he went down again, with Abram, just to help Bonatti bring up the bottles the next day. He went up and down until the 30th, when he developed phlebitis and stayed at Camp VIII. On the 29th I was at Camp VIII with Compagnoni, Bonatti and Gallotti. I was exhausted because I had made trail through the deep snow continuously for seven hours as

Compagnoni was not up to. There we made our plan for the final attack. We looked at the map and studied the mountain with binoculars and decided to put the tent of Camp IX beside the 'Bottleneck*', where there was a hump. We all agreed on that decision.

Is that where you actually set up Camp IX?
The 30th was a beautiful day, but I was still tired from the exertions of the previous day. Bonatti and Gallotti went down to Camp VII and then came back to Camp VIII where Gallotti remained. Abram also climbed up from Camp VII, and he continued with Bonatti and Mahdi towards the place we had selected for Camp IX. However, he had to stop and go back down to Camp VIII. Meanwhile, Compagnoni and I reached the place we had all agreed on for Camp IX. I said to Compagnoni, 'Shall we pitch the tent?' but Compagnoni said, 'No, here is no good, it's too dangerous'. He then suggested we cross over to the left. I said, 'Isn't it more dangerous that way?' But he wouldn't listen and so we carried on. At first I didn't think too much about the decision, but I didn't understand it. Then I said to Compagnoni, 'I'm going to untie myself, I don't trust this rock'. Eventually we reached a place that wasn't particularly good ... it was precarious with a bit of a slope. But I thought, 'Well, the others will get here before it gets dark, they'll manage'. Then we pitched the tent, but no one appeared.

But why do you think Compagnoni wanted to traverse to the left?
I only understood later ... I believe he didn't want Bonatti to reach us. When I saw Bonatti come towards us I asked Compagnoni why he didn't want him to reach us and he said that it was just the two of us that had to make the final climb to the summit.

---

* The 'Collo di Bottiglia' (literally 'Bottleneck') is a snow filled channel above 8,000 metres, that is bordered on the left (south) by the rocks climbed by Lacedelli and Compagnoni, and overhung by the enormous wall of ice which forms the lower part of the apex of K2. The Bottleneck, which looks like the easiest passage to the summit from lower down, was tackled by Lacedelli and Compagnoni only during the descent. On the ascent it was judged too dangerous and tiring because of the large amount of snow.

To me it didn't matter if it was the two of us, or another pair. If there had been four of us it would have been even better. So I told him that what he was saying was not a good idea, and that Bonatti would have been good additional support. But Compagnoni said that was not possible as there were only two oxygen carriers. I suggested we could take turns to use the oxygen, I even said that I was willing to climb without oxygen, but there was no changing his mind.

Let's not get too far ahead. You said that the afternoon passed but no-one arrived ….

At one point we saw three dots in the distance, but they were far away and I said to myself, 'They're not going to get here, they won't manage it'. It was at that point that I understood what Compagnoni had done. So I said to him, 'We should have pitched the tent down there.' But he said, 'No, it's better here'. 'No', I insisted, 'no!' But given the conditions it was obvious the camp would have been better down there.

Lino Lacedelli at 6,450m.

After a while I noticed that there were only two dots climbing up, Bonatti and the Hunza Mahdi. I found out later that Abram had had to go back. Bonatti was now close to the traverse, so I went out to talk to him. Compagnoni didn't want to come out of the tent. It was now obvious to me that since we had gone higher than anticipated Bonatti would have to leave the oxygen bottles somewhere below us, and that we would have to waste time needlessly the next day.

Did you manage to talk to Bonatti?
Yes, Bonatti was very upset of course and I understood why. But I didn't know what to say. How can you explain such a thing up there? At 8,000 metres it's difficult to talk anyway. After just a few words you start to cough. Bonatti said, 'Shine a light, I'm coming up'. I shouted out that it was too dangerous and that he shouldn't. The Hunza wouldn't have managed that traverse. What would have happened if he had fallen? It was dark and the traverse was really difficult. So I shouted to Bonatti, 'Don't come up, it's too dangerous. Go back to Camp VIII, leave the bottles where you are'. It needed a lot of time to explain. It was windy on the little ridge where we had pitched the tent, and I would start coughing after just two words. I also couldn't hear what Bonatti was saying very well and Mahdi was also shouting. So I said again, 'Leave the bottles, go back to Camp VIII'. Bonatti said, or at least I think he said, 'I can look after myself, but it's Mahdi …'. I thought he was concerned at not being able to reason with Mahdi, to explain the situation to him, not that he was afraid that they would not be able to climb down. I don't know what happened next. I said goodbye and returned to the tent. Afterwards I was told that Mahdi was so disoriented that he wasn't capable of climbing down to Camp VIII. He was suffering from mountain sickness, he hadn't acclimatised properly. At the time I was convinced they would climb down. Instead….

Back in the tent, did you discuss with Compagnoni what you had said outside?
Yes, I told him everything. I said that I had advised Bonatti to go down. 'You did well', he said, but at the time I didn't realise that he had another motive.

Camp VI. Compagnoni standing, with Bonatti and Rey sitting.

What was that?
While we were at Camp VIII we had decided that whoever was least tired, whoever was the fittest, would go up. Compagnoni had earache and wasn't feeling well. When we left Camp VIII he had said, 'You go on ahead, I'll follow later with the oxygen.' But in the end we all left together. If Bonatti had arrived with the Hunza it would have been impossible to bivouac with four in the tent. This was the point. Bonatti was certainly fit, more so than the two of us.

So you maintain that Compagnoni wanted to move Camp IX from the agreed position so that Bonatti wouldn't reach it. He was concerned at having to spend the night with four people in the tent and, worse, that he would be replaced by Bonatti who was in better physical condition?
Yes, but I understood this only much later. At that height you have no time to think too deeply. You think about going on, not about scheming. Up there it's difficult to think clearly. I just felt very bad when Bonatti arrived where Camp IX should have been.

Did you realise that Bonatti had spent the night out in the open?
I only realised in the morning when I saw someone through the
mist zig-zagging down. 'Who on earth is that?' I said to myself. So
I called out and the figure responded by raising his ice axe. It was
Bonatti. But where was the other one? It was then that I understood what had happened … I was really worried. I thought that
he would be very angry.

Bonatti assumed that we would have been lower down. I was
upset because obviously I was partly to blame, wasn't I? I can't say
I wasn't because I hadn't thought about what might happen. I
would have been happy if Bonatti and the Hunza had reached us.
The important thing for me was reaching the summit, either two,
or three, or four of us, it didn't matter. I wasn't so narrow-minded
that I was envious about the others. It wouldn't have worried me
even if Bonatti had taken my place. I wouldn't have felt offended,
although I might have tried to go up afterwards.

The next morning, while we were helping each other to put on
our crampons, we realised that we were starting to get frostbite in
our fingers. Then we went down to pick up the oxygen bottles, I
didn't want to get them, especially after I understood what had
happened the night before, so I said, 'Let's go back down'. I really
said that.

*But what alternatives were there that evening? How could the four of you
have sheltered in a tent* in which two people could only just fit?*
We can only speculate because that little tent was very low. The
way we were wrapped up, Compagnoni and I spent the night with
our legs stuck out of the tent because we couldn't completely fit in.

But if we had met Bonatti at 7,950 metres, where we had agreed
to put the tent, we would at least have been able to agree something together. I believe that the Hunza would probably have disappeared back down anyway because he wouldn't have been able
to carry on. He didn't have the right boots for high altitude. I am
not sure if he hadn't been given them, or if he wasn't wearing them
because he wanted to sell them. For three of us to sleep there we

---

* The 'Super K2' tent used in Camp IX was 200cm in length, 120cm wide at the front,
90cm wide at the back and 75cm high.

would have had to cut the tent, and then shelter the best we could. But the real problem would have been in the morning: who would have set off?

Do you think that Mahdi was attracted by the idea of getting to the summit? Was he promised anything?
I think that Bonatti had already told him there was a possibility of getting to the summit. I think he had promised him a reward, I don't know how many rupees or cigarettes, but there was also the promise of photos and articles in the newspapers. But Bonatti wasn't the only one who had promised things, everyone had said something about it when we were at Camp VIII. It was normal with the Hunzas. It was always necessary to encourage them in some way. The fact is, we were hoping that Abram would have been able to go up. I know they had spoken about it again at Camp VIII after Compagnoni and I had gone up. Anyway, when I saw Mahdi come up without using oxygen, I was impressed.

Do you think Bonatti wanted to get to the summit?
If only all four of us had been able to meet up at Camp IX … it's possible that Bonatti might have decided to go back. But finding himself in the situation he was in, he thought he had already been excluded.

And then, obviously all of us wanted to get to the summit. Bonatti had made a great effort, and I think he felt very fit. In that situation he felt excluded and naturally got upset. But what should I have told him, that afternoon, in those circumstances?

But the agreement with Bonatti was that he was bringing the oxygen up for you?
Bonatti had volunteered to bring up the bottles. But that's not to say he wouldn't have been able to make an attempt himself later. It was the fact that we pitched the Camp IX tent higher than we had agreed on that angered him so much. I agree with him on that. When we came down from the summit in the evening, at 11 o'clock, I wasn't happy and apologised to Bonatti, I explained to him and said, 'I'm really sorry, I wanted to stop where we agreed, but Compagnoni didn't want to'. Bonatti said to me, 'Don't worry, I'm not upset with you, but with him'.

Bonatti was accused, in Nino Giglio's article* in 1964, of having used up some of the oxygen, which was supposed to have been for you and Compagnoni, during the bivouac with Mahdi. Do you think it was possible that he used the oxygen? Do you think he wanted to get to the summit before you? Do you think that Bonatti had in mind, as Nino Giglio wrote, to play a cruel trick on you?

Absolutely not! Knowing Bonatti, that could never have been the case. When we agreed something between us that's how it was. And Bonatti wouldn't have been able to use the oxygen because we had the masks. How would he have managed it? But even if he had had the masks I am sure he wouldn't have used them because we had an agreement. Bonatti knew very well that the oxygen was needed for the highest part of the climb, for the final ascent. And Bonatti just wasn't the type to say one thing and do another: when he said something that was it. So what was said on that matter was a lie.

Those who accused Bonatti of having used the oxygen referred to the fact that the oxygen ran out before you arrived at the summit. Bonatti's defence was that the oxygen hadn't really finished before the summit, and he also questioned the time that you left Camp IX (and so the time that you started using the oxygen). According to Bonatti, it is not possible that you left between 4.00 and 4.30 as Compagnoni stated, because if you had you would have met him at his bivouac. Bonatti, who says he checked his watch, says that he left his bivouac a little after 6.00…

When we left the tent … I remember I saw Bonatti go down, so it was already daylight. I am not sure of the exact time. I didn't look at my watch, but it could have been between 6.00 and 6.30. I remember we weren't in the habit of looking at our watches. We were more interested in the weather. That morning we were a bit

---

* Nino Giglio published two articles in *Nuova Gazzetta del Popolo* (Turin, 26 July 1964 and 1 August 1964) in which he accused Bonatti of having tried to convince the Hunza Mahdi to attempt to reach the summit without telling Lacedelli and Compagnoni, of having abandoned Mahdi, by then frostbitten, at the bivouac, and of having used the oxygen intended for Lacedelli and Compagnoni during the night. Bonatti took legal action for libel against the journalist and obtained a judgement in his favour. Nino Giglio, on 5 March 1967, published another article retracting what he had said in the two preceding articles.

Cirillo Floreanini at 7,000m.

concerned because it was misty and the visibility was poor. The talk about 4.00 or 4.30 was certainly a mistake. We may have got up at that time, but we certainly left the tent much later. On the television, when Compagnoni spoke about the time we left, I confirmed it. As I have already said, on other occasions I also confirmed things that were not completely correct. But I didn't want to get into arguments, especially on television .... Anyway, it didn't seem particularly important to me. I remember I saw Bonatti from outside our tent, or rather I saw a person who afterwards was confirmed to be Bonatti, therefore it was already daylight. It was misty, but it was already light. We wasted a lot of time getting ready, fitting our crampons. At that height it was difficult to do anything quickly, you moved like a robot.

At the tent, we roped ourselves together, climbed up, traversed across and then went down again. It took us about an hour and a half to get to where the bottles were and then we were ready for the climb. We probably started towards the summit, breathing the oxygen, somewhat late. I can't be sure whether it was about 8.30 as Bonatti has written. I think we probably left for the summit at about 7.30. Anyway when we arrived at where the bottles were I said, 'What shall we do?' I wanted to leave everything there and go back down. I could see the bivouac that Bonatti had dug out of the snow and it made me feel really bad. I knew that they had survived, but I was afraid that they would have suffered bad frostbite. There was also the mist.

Who decided to set off?
Compagnoni. Noting his decision I picked up the oxygen bottles and set off. It took us three quarters of an hour to arrive back at the traverse. The snow was very deep. Above that, we first tried the gully to the right (the Bottleneck), but we sank deep into the snow. So then we tried the rocks on the left. First Achille tried, but he fell after a couple of metres. To stop him I had to throw myself across his path. Then I tried, after removing my crampons and gloves. It was a stretch of 30 metres of ice covered rock. The key to the summit….

I have heard grade 4 mentioned….
I don't know if it was grade 4, but the problem was the weight we were carrying. From the top of the pitch Achille led on up the snow: his pitch was longer, but less difficult. My glasses misted over and I had to take my gloves off to clean them. When I did, I noticed that my fingers were white and had lost all sense of feeling. We climbed another two rope lengths and the first oxygen bottle was finished.

Did you have rests during the ascent?
Yes, we would stop after every 30 metres. It was a strange way to climb. Often the second man would have to hammer in his ice axe so that it could be used as a step by the leader. And the second would always get covered in snow. Before each step you needed to get rid of the snow, take off your gloves, remove your glasses, clean them and then put your gloves back on. After a while the gloves were soaked, inside and out. I think that was the main reason for our frostbite.

Anyway, we carried on up the left side of the gully as the snow in the middle was still too deep to climb. We reached a place where we had to traverse further left beneath a huge wall of ice which looked as though it would fall on us at any moment. Then we reached the altitude at which Wiessner had stopped in 1939. About that time the second bottle of oxygen ran out. We continued round to the left, towards the south, on rocks where the climbing was easier. We stopped for a rest and then set off again, climbing a really steep section where, fortunately, the snow was firm....

Then, suddenly I found I couldn't breath and felt dizzy. I tapped on my back with my ice axe and asked Compagnoni if there was any oxygen left in the bottle. 'You've still got some', he said, but it clearly wasn't true. I looked at his – and it was empty like mine. So I told him he still had some as well. We were both afraid that the other would lose his nerve if he knew the truth. But the fact was that the oxygen was really finished and we were very scared. We had read before leaving Italy, that without oxygen it was not possible to survive for more than ten minutes above 8,500 metres. But we were feeling okay, even if it was hard to breath and our legs felt weak. I had wanted to remove the carrier with the oxygen bottles, but the problem was that in order to take it off I had to open a carabiner, and it was not possible with frozen fingers. So we decided to carry them to the top as a sort of proof that we had reached the summit. We also stayed roped together even though we didn't need to any more. If one of us had slipped he would have taken the other one down as well.

At what height was this?
Approximately 8,500–8,550 metres, but neither of us looked at the altimeter. When the oxygen finished I looked at the mountain to the south-east, 'That's Broad Peak,' I said, 'It's 8,047 metres high'. So my brain must have been working. But to check we started to discuss banal things, just to see if our minds were working clearly. My problem was that I felt as if I had a heavy load on top of my head, crushing it. I couldn't move any more. We tried to go on a few steps with the empty bottles. I felt a warm feeling in my legs, and then they went really cold. But my headache had gone and so I convinced myself that we could live a little longer. Then, just

when the oxygen had completely finished, we had an unexpected lift. The clouds parted and we saw five little specks at Camp VIII and it was as if they had given us a push upwards. Seeing them gave us courage. When you are up in the mountains there are no living creatures around you, so seeing a sign of life gives you encouragement.

Bonatti has protested that the photo on the summit shows pieces of ice on your beard, a sign that you had kept your oxygen mask on right up to the end. There is also a photo of Compagnoni at the summit with his mask still on. Bonatti, to refute the accusation of having used the oxygen during his bivouac the previous night, claims that the oxygen must still have been available even at the summit.

The oxygen in those bottles was too rich. It wasn't mixed very well like that in use today and it burned your throat breathing it. We were spitting out blood for two days after reaching the summit. Breathing was really painful. On some occasions Compagnoni would put on the mask, even when the oxygen was finished, because the air was less cold and less dry. The cold, dry air was very painful in the windpipe. Bonatti says I had ice on my beard – I know I had ice on my beard. He can say whatever he wants, but the truth is that the oxygen ran out *before* the summit. If only it had lasted all the way!

I know that it might seem strange that we didn't remove the bottles once the oxygen had finished, but we really couldn't … I would have willingly left them there and then. And then, after the oxygen had finished, the climb was less steep and we thought there wasn't far to go to the summit.

When did you know?

It became obvious. 'But … is that the summit?' I thought, 'I hope so'. So we linked arms and I said, 'Together'. At that point we looked at our watches. During the whole day that is the only time I can confirm, it was ten minutes before six o'clock. We were amazed that we had managed to get to the top after all the problems we had had, after our companions had fallen by the wayside, one by one. We thought, 'We'll be next', but instead…. We couldn't believe it, we were so pleased. On the summit the view was

Camp VII at 7,345 metres. In the background is Broad Peak.

astounding. After we had taken a few photos and shot a few reels of film we realised that it was getting late, and we were concerned about it getting dark.

Why did you link arms with Compagnoni, friendship or suspicion?
It was instinctive. I didn't want someone to say one day, 'Who was the first one to arrive?' In a football match it's the team who wins not the one who scores the goal. From a mountaineering point of view it's not important who arrives first. Neither of us had arrived there on his own, and the others had also played their part. They gave everything to enable us to get to the summit. This achievement was the work of the group, everyone in the expedition contributed. But the journalists never understand this. I knew that they would have asked, 'Who arrived first?', when we returned. As if it was a cycle race!

Were you able to think about this up there?
Yes, but not very clearly, it was more like instinct. At that height, without oxygen, you can't think properly, your head is full of confused thoughts. In the last stretch, Achille was convinced there was a woman behind him … and he was laughing. I also thought I had someone behind me, Guido Lorenzi. 'Surely he can't be there', I thought, 'Guido broke his leg'. Then it seemed like my fiancée was there, but I thought that she wouldn't have managed to get so high up. It took me a while, but then I understood that I was seeing the things I was thinking, as if my thoughts were becoming real. I also remember saying to Compagnoni, 'You can keep that woman, she might really be there … but I don't see any women, I only see my friends'.

Bonatti insists that the oxygen lasted as far as the summit in order to prove that he didn't use any during the bivouac. To sustain his view he did very precise calculations as to how long the oxygen should last….
Yes, but they are only theoretical calculations. At Base Camp Abram calculated that the German Dräger bottles that we were using should last ten hours. Possibly at 8,000 metres the Dräger might leak, or might last less. And then it's possible that we might have used more oxygen than we thought because of the altitude and the effort. Also, the mixture wasn't necessarily very precise.

Mario Fantin gave you a cine camera to film your arrival at the summit. Who did the filming?
Both of us. We took three reels. For the last one, which remained inside the camera, we placed ourselves in front of the camera while we shook hands and congratulated each other. The problem was that when we arrived back at Camp VIII we had a bit of a party. They removed our crampons for us and at that time I left the cine camera on the ground. During the night about 80 centimetres of snow fell, and we all forgot about the cine camera. I remembered when we had gone down. If someone wants to go and get it, it should still be there....

You took the film on the summit together, but then Compagnoni took CAI to court asking for compensation. He argued that his hands had been frostbitten because of the filming....
I thought that it was a rather petty thing. At one point he wasn't able to remove his gloves. It was very cold, and the glove was tight on his wrist. In my side pocket I had a penknife. I managed to take it out and open it with my teeth and I cut, and then removed, his glove. 'Give me a massage, give me a massage!' he shouted, 'How can I manage with frozen fingers?' he was saying, 'I've got a wife and two children ... How will I be able to work without these two fingers, how will I be able to look after my family? I'm going to bivouac here and go down tomorrow'. I told him not to think about his fingers and that to bivouac there would mean certain death. Then I put his right glove back on, but his left one flew away. Without thinking, I took off mine and gave it to him. In the end I brandished my ice axe, 'Down', I shouted, 'Now we go down'. It would have been a problem if one of us hadn't been in control. Fortunately Compagnoni got a grip on himself.

As usual, however, you encountered the greatest dangers during the descent....
It was dark, and I had a battery which was about to give up. The problem was that we couldn't go down the same way we had gone up because of our frozen hands. It would have been impossible. When we reached the traverse I went ahead. At the Bottleneck I

dug a hole, pushed my ice axe into the snow and wrapped the rope around it a few times. Then I pushed the ice axe in as far as it would go with my knees, because there was no strength left in my hands. I then made a sign to Compagnoni to go ahead, but he slipped and ended up falling 30 metres. If I hadn't secured him with the axe, just following my instinct, we would both have fallen down the Bottleneck. From there we carried on down the steep gully we had avoided during the ascent. We went one at a time, very cautiously, concerned that the snow would avalanche. After the traverse to Camp IX we let ourselves go down with a small avalanche. We were roped together. To slow the descent I used both the ice axe and my backside. At those heights your mind isn't working properly and you get a kind of false courage, nothing scares you.

When we arrived where we had left rucsacs we found a small bottle of cognac. We drank a few drops, but it hurt our throats and we quickly became drunk! We then carried on arm in arm and, after about 50 metres, we had to jump a crevasse, falling in a heap on the other side. I lost my ice axe. The crevasse was shaped like a bell – had we fallen in we would never have been able to get out. The problem was that we couldn't see our tracks any more. A little wind was enough to completely erase them. I remembered that we needed to go to the left, but we arrived at the top of a wall and we couldn't find the steps that we had made in the morning. Compagnoni went first, but suddenly I sensed the rope running away and I wasn't able to hold on to it because of my frozen hands. I thought, 'In a second it will go taut and pull me down as well'. I started to fall but instead came to rest a few metres from the top of a crevasse! The ice axe, which I had pushed into a crack, had held. Compagnoni had fallen into the snow up to his neck, but fortunately it was a V-shaped crevasse. Then I went down the left side, which was easier and a good decision. I also went flying at one point, but I only fell a few metres. Then, after another 100 metres, we picked up the tracks for Camp VIII. We started calling, shouting as loud as we could. Afterwards they told me that Pino Gallotti thought he heard something. 'You're dreaming', Abram said. But then they heard us. At that point I realised we were safe, that we had done it!

The Burden of K2

In the evidence used in the libel case against Nino Giglio, the Hunza Mahdi said that on his return to Camp VIII, Compagnoni was nice with Bonatti, but that Lacedelli and Compagnoni didn't say a word to each other. Why?

I was very angry with Achille. On the way down it had begun to dawn on me what had really happened at Camp IX. I didn't say very much to him. And Bonatti … for the record it was Bonatti who massaged my frostbitten fingers as soon as I got back. We didn't say too much, because my fingers were hurting a great deal, but I remember thanking him for what he had done. At the time there wasn't anything else to say. Then, as I've already said, Bonatti understood what had happened and had already said that he didn't hold it against me. I think that it's important to understand that Bonatti had made a great sacrifice. If you think about carrying the oxygen bottles up to 7,950 metres and then having to descend … what he did was exceptional and shouldn't be forgotten. I have never forgotten what he did. You see, in public I have spoken very little about what happened on K2. But on the few occasions that I have shown my slides I have always spoken well of Bonatti. I have always said that, without his sacrifice, the two of us would not have reached the summit.

All things considered, in your opinion, without the oxygen brought up by Bonatti, would you still have made it to the summit?
I don't know if we would have even tried … I've thought about it a lot. To speculate afterwards is always easy. Back then nobody thought that it would be possible to go to those heights without oxygen. But with hindsight maybe we would have made it. What is

certain is that we managed without oxygen at least from about 8,500 metres to the summit so…. Certainly it would have been much easier without the 18 kilos of oxygen bottles that we each carried. But then, by the same token, Bonatti could also have managed. He had acclimatised well and was in great physical condition.

On your return, the Pakistani press, and public opinion, complained about Mahdi's physical condition after the expedition. Ata Ullah, the official representative of the Pakistani Government, was the first to voice his disquiet. As a result, the report of Benedetto d'Acunzo, the Italian Consul in Pakistan, was written following the return of the expedition to Karachi, with the aim of establishing an official version of events. Ten years later, Nino Giglio's article, which was based on Pakistani sources and Compagnoni's testimony, accused Bonatti of having tried to beat you and Compagnoni to the summit. Writing about this, Robert Marshall said, 'His reaction (Ardito Desio's in 1954) to Ata Ullah's complaints was what would be expected from someone like him: he didn't hesitate in throwing Bonatti to the wolves. With a master stroke of diplomacy, he managed to heap all the blame on the irresponsible twenty-four year old mountaineer, and, since there were no legal issues involved, he was able to insist that the entire story was kept quiet in the interests of conserving friendly relations between Italy and Pakistan. He had probably promised Ata Ullah that he would punish the guilty one and we can't say that he didn't do it … the assumed guilty behaviour of Bonatti was hushed up in order not to harm the reputation of the expedition and of Desio himself. It was hushed up so well that even Bonatti remained ignorant until ten years later when the Giglio article appeared in Italy'[*] It is certainly a complex story. Do you also think that Bonatti was the sacrificial lamb?
I would say it went something like that, but I can't be completely sure. I haven't known about this for very long, and I certainly have no proof, but articles like that of Marshall have made me think. But whatever the case, the accusations made against Bonatti were absolutely false.

---

[*] The relevant Marshall comments are in the Bonatti books *Il Caso K2 40 anni dopo*, Ferrari Editrice, Clusone, 1995 and *K2, la verità. Storia di un caso*, Baldini Castoldi Dalai, Milano, 2003 which have not been translated into English, but see *The Mountains of My Life*, The Modern Library, New York, 2001 translated and edited by Robert Marshall, which covers the same ground.

Climbers on the lower part of the Abruzzi Spur.

The Pakistanis certainly wanted satisfaction and when Mahdi arrived home he obviously wanted to have his say. But in that position people often say what the authorities want them to say, and then the press open a hornet's nest. It seems to me, but I can't be sure, that Ata Ullah intervened when the arguments broke out on our return, and that he and Desio resolved the problem together. I don't know exactly how. Anyway, I remember something Compagnoni said on the 40th anniversary celebration, in 1994, when we went to Pakistan and met up with Mahdi. Compagnoni said to me, 'Let's hope Mahdi doesn't say anything'. 'Why?' I said, 'What could he possibly say?' I didn't understand at the time, but I understood a year ago. I understood many things ... but I can't prove them.

It's just an idea, but it seems a reasonable hypothesis that there was some sort of agreement between Desio, Compagnoni and Ata Ullah to blame Bonatti. They wanted to blame him for having forced Mahdi into going up to Camp IX. It is true that he pushed him, as all the others had done, but it was for a good reason and certainly not because he wanted to take the summit away from Compagnoni and myself.

Why did Compagnoni say, 'Let's hope Mahdi doesn't say anything?'
I didn't know then, and I don't really know now. 'What could he say?' I asked. We talked with Mahdi's son, who spoke English, while Compagnoni's wife translated into Italian. We found out that Mahdi was well enough. He had been a bit down, but now he was getting on okay. We spoke for a long time. He seemed really pleased to see us and he didn't say anything against anyone.

Should he have been annoyed with you because of the frostbite?
He didn't have the proper boots and that certainly wasn't our fault. If he had had boots like ours on, then nothing would have happened to him. Also, when we descended, Mahdi didn't come down with us as he should have done to begin immediately treatment for the frostbite. Instead he arrived the day after. Obviously in twenty-four hours the frostbite gets worse if it is not treated. I remember Pagani being very upset with Mahdi about that, but Mahdi hadn't thought about the frostbite. He, like all the other Hunzas, had thought more about carrying as much as possible down from Camp IV to Camp II, so that he could take it home. As a result he lost all his toes.

The day after he arrived, Mahdi was able to walk okay. I remember seeing him at Camp VIII. It seemed to be a relatively mild frostbite. Only the first part of the toes had gone black. It is possible that some of the toes might have been saved completely if he had gone down immediately with us to Camp IV.

How was the return for you?
As I said it snowed during the night. Next morning Compagnoni was complaining about his frostbite. I said that there was no point getting upset about it and the best thing to do was to concentrate

on getting down. We started down, but then Compagnoni disappeared. I was roped to Abram, Bonatti and Gallotti. I think Compagnoni was with one of the Hunzas. We discovered afterwards that he had fallen on his way down to Camp VII. He had stopped near a tent. He was okay, but a bit disoriented.

By the afternoon we had managed to get down to Camp IV. Pagani immediately gave us the first injections. It was very painful. The next day, 2 August, we arrived at Base Camp. On the way down, at Camp II we saw a Balti coming towards us: it was Birichin. He was out of breath and very emotional. After meeting us, he made some tea. He seemed like, he *was*, one of us, perhaps even better than us in some ways....

In the last part of the descent, below Camp II, there was a steep gully. I asked Abram to untie me and I went down on my backside and waited for the rest of them at the bottom. Then, above Base Camp, all the porters and the Hunzas came out to greet us, but Desio was nowhere to be seen.

I found myself behind Compagnoni when Desio finally met us, 'Ah, Achille', he said, 'I hear you managed it then', and embraced him. I was behind, with Abram, and after a while he finally noticed me. 'Ah, you as well Lacedelli', and he made as if to embrace me as well. 'I don't want your embrace,' I said. I remember thinking that I could have strangled him.

Talking of Desio, there is something I've not mentioned which explains why I was so angry. During the ascent, at Camp VIII, we couldn't make contact with Base Camp by radio, so we weren't able to tell them that we had reached 7,750 metres and established Camp VIII. That day, Desio was at 'Sella dei Venti'* on the left side of the mountain, looking down. Then, suddenly, we heard Desio on the radio. 'I haven't got time for you', he said, 'I need to get on with my studies'. So I insisted, 'But Professor, it's important that you listen so you can communicate with Base Camp'. He just got really annoyed. So I told him where he could go, and said, 'From now on, if you want to know what's going on you can come up and find out for yourself!' End of radio contact. I know that Desio spoke about

---

* The Skyang-La (Windy Gap), at 6,233 metres, to the north-east of K2 at the top of the Godwin-Austen Glacier.

On the ridge between Camps III and IV.

it afterwards at Base Camp. Angelino wrote down everything, he documented everything that was said, good and bad.

Angelino included this in his letter to the CAI Committee: 'There was no more reason to consider ourselves followers of a leader who had never really known us or had ever really tried to understand or get close to us, treating us with sourness, with no moments of friendliness or fatherly words, even though he often described himself as like a father to his "boys". He completely lacked the right mentality for the mountains. There is no other explanation for the way he gave his orders, and for his behaviour – as if he were a general, but a general who forgot that his men had not been called up for military service[*]

I remember when Desio arrived … it was about a hundred metres from Base Camp, perfectly groomed and shaved. We couldn't take

[*] Ugo Angelino, *Esposto ai membri della Commisione esecutiva del K2. The Monthly Journal of the Italian Alpine Club*, Turin, 1955, Vol. LXXIV, File 9-10.

him seriously. What kind of leader was he? They all went further than he did, half of the porters, the Baltis – Birichin had come up to Camp II just to bring us tea. The Hunzas at Base Camp all came out to greet us, but not Desio!

When we were all finally reunited at Base Camp, Desio immediately told us not to speak to the newspapers. He specified a time, but I don't remember how long. He said that he was the only one who should speak to the press. Then he said that we should hand over the photos that we had taken at the summit to CAI, to the vice-president Amedeo Costa. However, before handing them over I made copies for myself. He also asked us to give him our diaries. We discussed this among ourselves. Compagnoni said that he would hand his over. We asked Pagani for his advice and in the end decided not to hand over anything. We agreed that for a very simple reason: he would have written what he wanted. During the expedition I was considered the last wheel on the wagon, the most unimportant of the climbers, so there was no way he would have taken much notice of my version of events. As a result of our decision, Desio's book lacks any detail of what happened between Camp II to Camp VIII, the sequence of movements, and the work that the group did. This is because Compagnoni wasn't with us and Desio's book, which has become the 'official' version of the expedition, was only based on Compagnoni's diary.

Immediately after your return to Base Camp a quarrel broke out between Desio and Fantin because movie film had run out. There was then a long legal wrangle....*

Yes, Desio took legal action against Fantin. Zanettin, one of the geologists, had taken three or four boxes of film of the type that

---

* On 7 August 1954, Mario Fantin wrote in his diary, '(Desio) was surprised that there was no 16mm film left for the scientific expedition. I told him that the film had run out a while ago and that I was surprised at his request, as I hadn't expected it.... I was sorry that I couldn't grant his wish, but the position was clear: the 'official' quantity of film had been used, together with an additional 500 metres of my own private supply. I had to return some reels of Angelino's personal stock. If it was not possible to document his scientific investigations it was not my fault. Professor Desio seemed bothered that I had so robustly rebutted his complaints in front of the others. However we are so used to such things from the leader that we are no longer bothered.'

Desio needed without saying anything to the Professor. Zanettin took the film and Desio blamed Fantin. Those of us who had been with Fantin knew that he couldn't have taken the film. When Zanettin returned he said, 'Oh Professor, excuse me, I took the boxes'. The mystery was solved but still, out of pride, Desio wouldn't admit his error, and even took Fantin to court following our return to Italy. He wouldn't let it go – Fantin had to be to blame. When we returned to Italy we had to visit the Pope and the President in Rome. Before meeting President Einaudi we were all together in a room with Desio, and Pagani spoke for us all. He said 'You must apologise to Fantin, because you have offended and insulted an innocent man'. In the end Desio had no choice but to apologise and withdraw the action, because it was a false accusation.

Following your return to Base Camp you were unable to really enjoy your victory….
Well, we were all euphoric. After three days we had a little party. We drank some cognac, but we only needed a small amount and we were drunk! Just looking at the bottle made you feel queasy, I don't think it was very good for us at that height.

I wasn't well because of the terrible pain in my hands. First I was in the tent with Fantin, then Bonatti came to help me. He stayed up with me for two entire nights after which I began to recover. It was so painful I didn't know what I was doing. Sometimes I found myself out on the glacier at night not knowing how I got there. Bonatti would come and take me back to the tent. But the pain was important because I knew that I was getting over the frostbite.

But how did you actually get the frostbite? Was it when you took the film without gloves as Compagnoni said?
That's complete rubbish! We had to take our gloves off because they were too tight on our wrists. We took them off with a penknife and the tips of our crampons. Compagnoni said that his fingers were frozen because of his shooting the film when he was on the summit. That's certainly not true. We started getting frozen fingers

when we were putting on our crampons at Camp IX and it just got worse further up. We were continually having to take off our gloves to clean our glasses. As a result we both ended up with gloves that were wet on the inside, and when the temperature fell the inside of the gloves got frozen. But Compagnoni's frostbite wasn't as bad as mine. Nine of my fingers were affected and only two or three of his. After I gave Achille my glove when we were on the summit I only had the inner silk one left. Fortunately my circulation was good and I recovered well.

Weren't you tempted to go to court with CAI because of the film?
No, for the love of God, that was all rubbish! When you are with a colleague and he needs help, you help him. In my opinion Compagnoni made a mistake. If it had happened to me and Compagnoni had given me his glove, I would have thanked him publicly. But he has never said anything. On the contrary, he was doing an interview with a journalist, I can't remember which newspaper, who asked him if he had helped Lacedelli, if he had pulled him to the summit. I'm not saying that Compagnoni actually answered yes, but he was certainly ambiguous. The end of the article said, 'Compagnoni will never reveal how he dragged the exhausted Lacedelli …'. How can they write such things?

The morning after the article was published I received two telegrams, one from the CAI and one from vice-president Costa which said, 'Don't say anything I beg you'. Then Bibi Ghedina and Claudio Apollonio arrived at my house, really furious. They wanted to send our CAI cards back to Milan in protest. 'Don't worry, I'll sort it out,' I said, 'I'll go to Milan myself'. So I went to the clinic in Milan where Compagnoni was recovering. When he saw me he said, 'Oh Lino, I'm really sorry'. I said, 'Don't play the innocent,' to which he said 'Should I send my wife and son outside?' I said 'No, they can stay. If you said what they printed then you are really a rat!' Those were my precise words. I added 'You know very well what happened. You should never say things like that, we shouldn't be in two different camps'. I don't believe he actually said what was written, but he had been ambiguous. He had the same attitude with Bonatti.

So he never retracted his words? He never apologised?
Yes, of course, there were three lines of denial in the same newspaper, signed by the same journalist! Three lines!*

I think we're talking about the article in Epoca *magazine. Regarding that article there's a quote in the Saglio report to the Milfan Council of CAI on 27 October 1955. I'll read you an extract: 'In the session of 10 October 1954 the* Epoca *article came to our attention, which, with a large headline, said that Compagnoni had dragged Lacedelli to the summit of K2. The article provoked the justified anger of the people of Cortina and Tissi spoke about it. Desio assured the Commission that he would find the people responsible and that he would request an exemplary punishment. Dr Lombardi would assist. I was later informed who the source was for this pantomime, for the article being written, directly from the office of* Epoca *in the presence of foreign journalists, and it was also confirmed by diverse sources. It was a person very close to Desio. The correction never came, and the punishment never happened'.** Do you know anything about this?*
No, but it doesn't upset me any more. During the first years I used to get very bothered. I remember when the journalists came to my house I would say to my aunt, 'Say I'm not here, I'm going to the barn to sleep'. I didn't want to see anyone. They talked so much nonsense … what they wrote depended more on whether they liked a particular person or not. Often they knew next to nothing about mountaineering. I remember one of them writing that K2 was short for 'kilometre two'! Can you imagine, a big headline saying 'Kilometre Two'.

Someone told me that Compagnoni wrote, 'If Lacedelli hadn't been there I don't know if I would have made it to the top'.
Yes, that was last year. A little article. After forty-eight years…. Anyway these matters haven't bothered me very much. When you are in a roped party and your companion is in trouble, you help him if you can. That's what I did and I'm happy to have done it. I

---

* It should, however, be remembered that Compagnoni, in a brief passage published in the Milan edition of the newspaper *Il Corriere della Sera*, resolutely denied the article in question while he was recovering in the clinic.

** *The Monthly Journal of the Italian Alpine Club*, Turin, 1955, Vol. LXXIV, File 9-10.

30 July. Compagnoni (seen here) and Lacedelli unroped for the traverse to the site of Camp IX.

know that I led on the key 30 metres in mixed conditions on the final stretch above 8,000 metres. Compagnoni was doing okay, he just had a momentary crisis. Anyway, notwithstanding the lies written by the press I'm happy that we both managed to get down. Imagine what they would have written if I had returned on my own ... perhaps that I had murdered him! If you think about the friction between those from the Western Alps and those from the Dolomites ... the journalists wouldn't have thought twice. And it's true that there was a certain rivalry, though it came mostly from the Westerners who tended to look down on us. For me, if my companion was Russian or Japanese or English, it wouldn't have made any difference. A man is a man and that's all. If you're together he is your companion and you must support him. What happens afterwards is unimportant.

Talking about the rivalry, Robert Marshall insisted that there was bad feeling between yourself and Bonatti ever since you and Bibi Ghedina had climbed his route on the Gran Capucin* in a day.
No, no, no, I know that's been said. We went at it hard** and there's nothing strange in climbing in one day a route that's been opened up needing bivouacs. Logically on the second ascent you use the pitons fixed by the first ascent party. The next time you can high step in your *etriers* and use fewer pitons. You can even use one where they used five or six the first time. It is also the case that climbers from the Dolomites are more used to vertical faces and fixing difficult pitons. Anyway Bibi and I weren't trying to undervalue Bonatti's route. On the contrary, it was a very impressive route, even the part after the ledge, the final part, had difficult sections. Bonatti and I always got on well together. I have already said that we did the Direttissima on the Cinque Torri together.

---

* 'As for Lacedelli, he was already not too well disposed to Bonatti, as evidenced by his lightning second ascent of Bonatti's route on the east face of the Grand Capucin in 1951' (Robert Marshall in his *What really happened on K2?*, in Walter Bonatti's *The Mountains of my Life*, The Modern Library, New York, 2001 translated and edited by Robert Marshall).

** Bonatti and Ghigo had taken four days to open the route. Lacedelli and Ghedina repeated it in a day: fifteen successive ascents were necessary for a second repetition without bivouac.

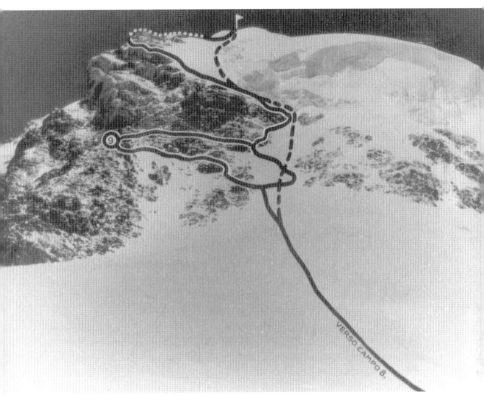

*The route to the summit, with the position of Camp IX and the
traverse to it marked. The dashed line is the more direct route taken
by Compagnoni and Lacedelli on the descent.*

*And during the expedition, before the events surrounding Camp IX was
there anyone who didn't get on well with Bonatti?*
Desio. But not only with Bonatti. It was the same with Abram and
myself. If there was anything that needed saying we would say it
clearly. Desio didn't like it when we debated his orders. But I think
that even someone like me has the right to be heard sometimes.
Even though I was considered little more than a porter – at least I
managed to achieve something. If ever we said anything, myself,
Bonatti, Abram and the others, our views were never considered.

Only Desio's and Compagnoni's views mattered and their word was law. The rest of us....

You say that Bonatti was the victim of an injustice. Was that more because of the events at Camp IX, or because of what happened afterwards back in Italy with the press?

I would say afterwards. The final part of the ascent we did together. We spoke about it afterwards and I think we reached an understanding. What happened to Walter was unpleasant, but it could have happened to anyone. I think he suffered the real injustice later, and I think that had more of an effect on him. I cannot but agree with him.

Would you like to meet him? Do you think that the fiftieth anniversary will be an opportunity?

I really hope so. I think we just need time. In life things change....These years of arguments haven't made anything better and I'm sorry for that. It would be good to get together. He was always an affable guy, with a cheerful disposition....

After your return to Italy, from the first celebrations until today, you have always kept yourself away....

After K2 Compagnoni returned to Italy by plane. He went with Pagani, Rey and Fantin who had other commitments. The others said, 'Why don't you go with Compagnoni?' 'To do what?' I asked, 'He is going to be honoured'. 'Don't you want me with you?' I said, 'I would be happy to go back with you'. So I went back with the others by ship and spent eleven fabulous days. We had a great time on board. Getting back first didn't matter to me. Compagnoni went back to be seen, but also because of his frostbite. My frostbite had stopped. There was no problem waiting a while, so....

Did the amputation of your thumb take place in Pakistan or Italy?

In Cortina, at the Institute Codivilla-Putti. Compagnoni went to a plastic surgeon, despite Pagani having advised him to go to Turin where there was a specialist. According to Pagani, if he had gone there he would only have lost the first section of his little finger. Afterwards Pagani said that Compagnoni's surgery had not been

Lacedelli fixing his crampons at Camp IX on the morning of 31 July.

done correctly. He was left with two stumps that are still very sensitive to the cold.*

Who have you kept on good terms with over the past years?
Everyone! All of us, except Bonatti, would see each other every year in the autumn, apart from last year. The reunion would always take place in a different place. At Angelino's house, at Compagnoni's, at Abram's ... we would have one or two days of party with much laughing and joking.

We are at a moment of balance. Thinking back, is there anything you regret? A mistake that you wouldn't repeat?
With the benefit of hindsight, the oxygen! I wouldn't carry it up for anything. I will never forget the weight of those 18 kilos, plus all the other equipment. That would be a lot here, but up there it was a terrible burden.

Also ... well, I regret not having climbed anywhere else outside the Alps. When we returned from K2, Floreanini, Abram and the rest of us planned to ask for permission to climb Broad Peak and the Mustagh Tower. But Professor Graziosi, who had been part of the scientific expedition, had been given some military maps of the region. He was supposed to have sent them back but he didn't. As a result, Italy was excluded from being given permission for expeditions, I don't remember whether it was for four or five years. So I said to myself, 'I can't go on living off my siblings, I must do something'. So my brother Leo and I opened a shop, K2 Sport. At the beginning I ran it by myself, then we formed a company. Now our families run it.

Did you ever think how your life might have been without K2? What would you have done?
I think I would have got used to working as I did before ... a blacksmith or something like that.

---

* Compagnoni was operated on by the surgeon Gustavo Sanvenero Rosselli. The flesh of Compagnoni's fingers was stripped, then the whole hand was placed in a 'pocket' created in the live flesh of his abdomen and left there until the flesh fused with his fingers. The hand was then detached from the pocket and the fingers remodelled.

Would you say that K2, after 1954, became a millstone around your neck?
Yes, but I always tried to stay away from the controversy. There have been so many arguments and articles over the years and the journalists have written just about everything they possibly could. I tried to stay out of it all so as not to ruin the memories of everything that we achieved. We didn't climb K2 by sitting around a table with journalists. We actually went there. One of us didn't return. Our sacrifices were real, and these things cannot be changed on paper.

The story is important though. Don't you think it's time to rewrite the story of K2?
After about fifteen years all of us climbers decided we would write a book together. It was started off by Gallotti, Angelino and Pagani. I sent my contribution to Gallotti who made a few changes. But we were missing contributions from Compagnoni and Desio. So we were unable to complete it. The book which Desio wrote was incomplete. It said very little about what really happened. We wanted to write a book together so that everyone could tell the story from his point of view. A book which collected together all the individual contributions would have been important. That's what we said to Desio, but he wanted to 'administer' our contributions to suit himself.

In January 1955 all the climbers except Compagnoni and Viotto signed a letter protesting about Desio's first book. The letter expressed concern about the episode regarding the film, deploring the Desio–Fantin problem. Why didn't Compagnoni want to sign the letter?
Compagnoni was too close to Desio. He had written his own little book[*] which included things that I would never have written. For example, when the poor fellow was talking about how he couldn't work any more without his fingers, how he wouldn't be able to provide bread and cheese for his family. Things to make people cry.

---

[*] Achille Compagnoni, *Uomini sul K2*, Veronelli Editore, Milano, 1958.

31 July 1954. Achille Compagnoni (above) and Lino Lacedelli
(right) on the summit of K2.

We're just not able to finish the story without falling into the same old arguments....
Well, there have been so many incidents, like the story of the Columbus prize that we were awarded in Genoa. The prize was a caravel with silver rigging, and was awarded to the best sportsmen in the world. Compagnoni wasn't there because he was in hospital. Genoa's Mayor, Vittorio Pertusio, was to present us with the caravel, a spectacular trophy. 'So', the Mayor said to me, 'I will give it to you and you must pass it on to Desio'. When he gave it to me, I held on to it for a little while, until I saw Desio stretching his arms to take it. In a sudden flash of inspiration, I turned and gave it to the President of CAI .... All my friends jumped to their feet in surprise. Later, Desio asked to have the trophy for himself and his Institute. 'This belongs to me', he said and he took it and kept it for a long time.

Wasn't there also a dispute between Desio and CAI regarding a lack of transparency in the accounts of the expedition?
Nothing unusual. In Pakistan, when we came back from K2, there were still 7 million lire on deposit, for the use of the expedition. The money was in Desio's name. I didn't have a cent. That was of no great importance to me, though it would have been nice to have been able to buy something as a souvenir of the expedition. I was like some vagabond, and vice-president Costa, who knew me, said, 'Lino, do you need any cash', 'No, no, I'm okay', I replied. I was embarrassed to say yes. 'Shall I advance you 300 rupees?', he insisted. 'Yes, okay then', I said in the end. I bought a rug that I still have in my house, hanging on the wall, and a few things to give to my family. As far as I know, of all the money that was supposed to be for the use of the expedition, no-one was able to touch a single lira. I don't know what Desio did with it. Anyway, Costa was an exceptional person. Rey and Viotto were also short of money, and Costa gave them something as well. He never asked for the money back. He contributed a lot of his own money to that expedition, but in the end Desio treated him like a doormat.

I know it's not nice to hear such things, but it's better to talk

Left:
Colonel Ata Ullah addresses the Balti porters during one of the numerous 'strikes' that took place throughout the walk-in to K2.

Below:
Erich Abram and Ubaldo Rey pause among apricot trees ladened with blossom during the walk-in.

Porters on a steep section of the walk-in.

Above: Bivouac at Urdukas.

Below: Walk-in camp below the Towers of Biacedi.

Above: Base Camp.

Left: Camp at 4,447 metres during the walk-in.

Below: Achille Compagnoni.

Above: Porters arriving at Base Camp.

Right: Installing the cable lift which was used to transport equipment from Camp I to Camp II.

Above: Lino Lacedelli at a camp on the Baltoro Glacier.

Right, above: Looking towards Mitre Peak from Camp IV.

Right, below: Camp IV with Masherbrum beyond.

Above: Achille Compagnoni climbing the Black Pyramid between Camps VI and VII.

Right: Walter Bonatti and Sergio Viotto approaching Camp VII.

Above: 28 July. Ubaldo Rey and Lino Lacedelli prepare to set out for Camp VIII.

Right: Forcing a trail for a few metres through deep snow, then returning to recover his rucsac, Lacedelli led all the way from Camp VII to Camp VIII during the summit attempt.

Left, above: Camp VII at 5am with Broad Peak in the background.

Left, below: Camp VIII at 7,630 metres.

Below: Lino Lacedelli on the way to Camp IX.

The summit of K2.

Compagnoni (left) and Lacedelli (right) at Base Camp after their summit climb.

about them. I have never said these things to the journalists because … because I couldn't say them then. I'm not saying that Desio didn't have some merits, obtaining the permission for the expedition, and general organisation. He achieved a lot, although the organisational work that Angelino did is often forgotten. It was just that Desio's behaviour towards us … he didn't care about our sacrifices and the risks that we took. He might be a great Professor, but as a human being … and that's the truth.

Part 3

A Story to Rewrite

Reconsidering the Myth

The interview with Lino Lacedelli is both moving and thought provoking. Not just because his answers offer a unique insight, but also because of the clarity and harshness of many of his comments.

The first thing that must be done is to compare what he says with what has been produced previously. But where should we start? Firstly, of course, with the official account imposed by Desio in his book (and the effective block on the climbers telling their own story). What Desio writes is not a story of the expedition, but a chronology, a chronology warns Lacedelli, that is full of gaps and inaccuracies. There were only two sources for the book: Compagnoni's diary and Desio's own point of view, the latter with the proviso that Desio was nearly always a long way away from the action.

Apart from the facts and the events he brings to life, what is new about Lacedelli's story is his portrayal of the atmosphere in which the expedition took place following its departure from Italy. An atmosphere in which there was a constant tension between the climbers and the expedition leader. There was a continual lack of understanding, with episodes when the entire expedition was at risk, to put it in nautical terms, of either mutiny or shipwreck. The climbers' camaraderie and spirit of survival – from Desio even more than from K2 – allowed them to overcome the expedition's moments of crisis. To this should be added the sense of duty, the calmness and reserve which formed part of the character of those eleven Italians who became part an extraordinary historical adventure. Today it would be hard to find a group of climbers who would allow themselves to be treated in the way Desio treated his 'boys'. Long before Lacedelli's interview, the poor relationship between Desio and the climbers had already been alluded to by the journalist Fulvio Campiotti in his book *K2*, and by Mario Fantin, the expedition's film-maker, in his *K2: Sogno Vissuto*.

Another potentially embarrassing theme of Lacedelli's account is the relationship between the climbers and the local population, in their role as porters. Even today it is popular to portray the indigenous population of these mountain areas as 'well meaning savages', generous and smiling, lacking material possessions, but rich in spirituality: people from whom we Westerners can recapture lost values. The insight that Lacedelli, a mountain dweller himself, has given us into the Hunzas and Baltis is neither edifying nor, above all, 'politically correct'. Among the porters who formed that long procession to the mountain there was certainly no lack of affable and admirable characters, but it seems from his account that most of them were loafers and liars, always ready to claim illness and to run away at every opportunity after pilfering something from the climbers. Lacedelli recalls that, on occasions, 'it was necessary to take one or two aside and show them the ice axe', and it is interesting to note the fairness with which Desio treated the porters in comparison to his harsh treatment of the climbers. The observations of Lacedelli range in shade from white to black, from the cheerful to the sad, when he reflects on Mahdi's frostbite, the inducements given to the Hunzas to persuade them to continue up the Abruzzi Spur, the ambiguous relationship between Desio and Ata Ullah, and Pakistani public opinion. In the background there is always the Bonatti issue, victim or sacrificial lamb, a constant presence in every recollection of the Italian K2 expedition.

And since Bonatti's name has been raised, it is time to confront Desio's account of the final summit climb in his official book. Desio attributes the story to Lacedelli and Compagnoni, or, at least, that is what he says in a note at the bottom of the page. We know that neither Lacedelli, nor Compagnoni actually wrote this account. Today, Lacedelli says 'they probably made me sign it', and remembers the interview with Dino Buzzati from which the account might have been taken (in the same way that Guglielmo Zucconi, after having gathered the material, was the 'actual' writer of Compagnoni's book *Uomini sul K2*). At that time Dino Buzzati was working for *Corriere della Sera*, and the account that was published in Desio's book had appeared previously in the newspaper in two instalments, on 21 and 25 November 1954. The fact that a note indicating that copyright for the articles belonged to the newspaper, which appeared at the end of the account, makes one think that they were effectively written by Buzzati. That said, however, the brief introduction to the first instalment, written in italics, could be seen as supporting a different view. It noted that, 'Professor Desio, the expedition's leader, who prepared this account some time ago, has authorised its use as a source'. What exactly does 'prepared this account some time ago', and 'authorised its use as a source' mean? If it means that the text came from Desio, then why did *Corriere* have the copyright? Does it actually mean merely that Desio had authorised Lacedelli and Compagnoni so Buzzati would write it for the newspaper?

Whatever the source of the text, it is clear that the report which Lacedelli signed is inconsistent with the events as stated in this interview. The 1954 account, in comparison to the one he has given now, lacks detail and is different in many areas. The 'Bonatti question' does not require further discussion in the official version, since that account does not deal with the reason for the change in position of Camp IX. At this point we should remember that Lacedelli now admits to having signed several versions of the story that were not completely accurate. 'My major concern was avoiding involvement in the media controversy', he admits today. 'That was why, sometimes, I confirmed things even when I knew that they hadn't happened exactly like that.'

But why was Lacedelli unable to impose his story on Compagnoni? As we have seen, Compagnoni was Desio's favourite, and, as we are now aware, with the benefit of what we have learnt from Lacedelli's interview, Compagnoni's merits and opinions were emphasised, in comparison to those of Lacedelli, in the official account: in support of this, just read through the account of what happened on the morning of the final ascent, when the two climbers arrived where the oxygen bottles had been left by the unfortunate Bonatti and Mahdi. 'The weather seemed to be deteriorating. The mist was slowly rising, in a little while it would envelop us completely. A few snowflakes fell. "What do you say?" asked Lacedelli. And Compagnoni – whom Desio had made responsible for the attack on the summit – replied without hesitation: "I say we ought to have a try"'. If it is true that Lacedelli signed such an account, he must have assumed that there was no alternative.

But we should return to the Bonatti affair, because, clearly, that is the main reason for the controversy still surrounding the K2 expedition. We will deal with the contested elements of the story in detail, one by one, comparing the official version with the new elements offered by Lacedelli's story.

The Position of Camp IX

'At about 4.30pm we emerged on the slope above the ice wall, anxious to know what awaited us above. But before even taking in the view of the summit that was by now close, the route to it visibly free from surprises, we called out to our companions. They heard us and answered. But where was their tent?' These words, taken from Walter Bonatti's account, mark the start of the drama of Bonatti and Mahdi's bivouac on the night of 30 July after they had carried the oxygen for Compagnoni and Lacedelli up to the previously agreed point. What exactly had happened?

Having reached the high slope, the two lead climbers had begun a long traverse to the left, over difficult, smooth rocks. Compagnoni justifies this in his book by saying that they were escaping from the threat of seracs falling from the final summit pyramid. But Lacedelli disagrees that this was a plausible motive, saying that in his opinion the risk of that traverse to the left was much greater than the risk of an avalanche from the frightful formation of seracs, which, as stated even in the Compagnoni–Lacedelli account in Desio's book, threatened them throughout the whole of the traverse.

In the present interview, Lacedelli, for the first time, says that there was an argument that continued in the tent, about that decision between himself and an immovable Compagnoni. The pair would have to reverse the traverse the following morning in order to get back on to the line of ascent. It was a pointless traverse which, Lacedelli recalls, resulted in them going higher and more to the left than necessary, and made them waste two hours in total. (The camp was at an uncertain altitude: in his official book Desio puts it at 8,050 metres, but at 8,080 metres in the photo of the Spur;

Compagnoni puts it at 8,100 metres in his book; Bonatti places it at 8,150 metres based on his assessment of 8,100 metres for the height of his and Mahdi's bivouac.)

Lacedelli remembers in this interview that he refused to remain roped to Compagnoni and reached the site chosen for Camp IX on his own. Once in the tent, pitched in an incomprehensibly awkward position, and certainly no less dangerous than the position that had been agreed (at a height of 7,900–7,950 metres according to Bonatti), both of them heard Bonatti's shouts for assistance. By now night had fallen, and Compagnoni left Lacedelli to go out to talk to Bonatti. From Compagnoni's stubbornness in insisting on undertaking the traverse, and his apparent satisfaction at hearing that Bonatti and Mahdi had given up the attempt to reach the tent, Lacedelli makes a clear accusation against his companion: Compagnoni had intentionally fixed the camp far away from the line of ascent and in such an awkward position in order to prevent Bonatti and Mahdi from reaching it.

And the motive? The fear of having to spend the night with four men in one small tent, and the fear of being joined or even replaced by Bonatti the following day for the final climb to the summit. Supporting evidence for this comes from the conversation between the two men in the tent, in which Compagnoni explicitly stated that he and Lacedelli should be the ones to make the final climb and not Bonatti. Lacedelli does not have objective evidence to back up his theory, but how could he? We are talking about words and intentions between two mountaineers, alone at 8,000 metres. But the testimony of Lacedelli is, nevertheless, an authoritative one and his account finally, after fifty years, gives a precise explanation to that senseless traverse and that 'misplaced' camp.

The Alarm Clock for the Summit

LA VOLPE: Which one of you said, 'Okay, let's go....'?
COMPAGNONI: Ah no, both of us together. That was a decision taken, taken together....'
LA VOLPE: So you left the tent at approximately four o'clock?
COMPAGNONI: Um ... four o'clock, half past four.
LACEDELLI: About four, half past four.

This exchange took place in a *Special Tg1* news programme conducted by Alberto La Volpe on the Rai 1 television channel, which went out in the evening of 30 July 1984, to celebrate the thirtieth anniversary of the first ascent of K2. It is the first and only time that Lacedelli was quoted giving the time that the summit pair left Camp IX on the morning of 31 July 1954. According to the account in Desio's book, after retracing the traverse and descending to the point where Bonatti and Mahdi had left the oxygen bottles, Compagnoni and Lacedelli set off for the summit. The time they set off, and hence the time that they started to use the oxygen, was stated to be about 06.15. Walter Bonatti, accused in 1964 in the *Nuova Gazzetta del Popolo* of having used some of the oxygen during his and Mahdi's bivouac, has paid a lot of attention to the precise timings of that morning. He had already noted in his court action against Nino Giglio that the oxygen should have lasted around ten hours, which was compatible with a departure of 06.15 and the oxygen running out a little after 16.00 (the time declared by Compagnoni).

Later Bonatti, after consulting an almanac giving sunrise times for the position of K2, and considering the fact that Compagnoni and Lacedelli, after having just left the tent on the morning of 31 July, saw a climber far away (Bonatti himself), concluded that the two could not have left their tent at between 04.00 and 04.30 as they had stated in the television interview. To do this they would have had to have put on their crampons in the dark, and what is more Bonatti on his way down to Camp VIII would have been invisible. To complicate (or simplify) this matter, in 1995 the Australian Robert Marshall found two photos of the climbers on the summit of K2 in a copy of *Mountain World* magazine of 1955. In these images, he noted, Compagnoni was wearing his oxygen mask, and Lacedelli had pieces of ice on his beard. The latter was, concluded Marshall, a sign that Lacedelli had just taken his mask off.

For Walter Bonatti, there could only be one conclusion: he could not have consumed Compagnoni's and Lacedelli's oxygen. Primarily, this was because he did not have a mask to do so. But also because the two climbers could not have set off for the summit before 08.30 and so the oxygen could not have run out before they had reached the summit, as the official report had maintained. Although initially providing arguments in his own defence, these calculations soon became an accusation against the official version of the story, which, with respect to the oxygen story, was clearly false.

During the interview for this book Lino Lacedelli admitted making a mistake in stating that the time of departure was between 04.00 and 04.30. Even though he remembers not having looked at his watch, he has since calculated the time, taking account of the dawn light, of having seen Bonatti going down, and the time the pair had taken to put on their crampons, climb to where the oxygen bottles had been left and to prepare themselves ready to leave. According to Lacedelli, the time that they set off for the summit is not compatible with that given in the official story (06.15), but nor is it compatible with that suggested by Bonatti (around 08.30). Lacedelli concludes that the oxygen taps were opened at around 07.30. He admits that he confirmed 04.30 as being the time that they left the tent in order not to cause a stir by contradicting Compagnoni in the television studio. In defence of Lacedelli, it should be noted that he was nervous and embarrassed in front of the television cameras, and was simply confirming a time that had been stated by Compagnoni. And it must not be forgotten that the timings of events at the start of the summit climb only became an issue a year later when, with his book, *Processo al K2*, Bonatti laid the foundations for his defence entirely on this point. With the benefit of hindsight one can conclude that Lacedelli should have been more careful in confirming something that was incorrect even if, at the time, it was not a significant detail.

Apart from the arguments set down above, there is actually proof of the inaccuracy of Compagnoni's statement on the time of departure from Camp IX – and the proof comes from Compagnoni himself:[*] it is the photo he took of Lacedelli on the morning of 31 July just outside the Camp IX tent. In the picture, which is included in this book, but which has already been published elsewhere, Lacedelli is pictured putting on his crampons. The almanac for 31 July 1954 at the position of K2, as Bonatti discovered years ago, states that the sun rose that morning at 04.54. Compagnoni maintained that they left the camp between 04.00 and 04.30, which meant that the two men must have put on their crampons even earlier. It is impossible that such a sharp photo (a sign of a relatively short exposure) could have been taken in twilight. In addition, the glow around Lacedelli is compatible with the 06.00 to 06.30 he indicated in the interview for this book.

To the accusations made against Bonatti in 1964 that he tried to get to the summit before them, and of having used the oxygen, Lacedelli has responded categorically, almost refusing to discuss the technical details. For Lacedelli, Bonatti is above all suspicion, and not only because of timings, masks and mixers. 'Even if he had had the masks', says Lacedelli, 'I am sure he wouldn't have used them because we had an agreement. Bonatti knew very well that the oxygen was needed for the highest part of the climb, for the final ascent. And Bonatti just wasn't the type to say one thing and do another: when he said something that was it. So what was said on that matter was a lie.'

Where Lacedelli parts company with Bonatti, however, is the issue of the oxygen running out before the summit. He has confirmed the details here, indicating 8,500-8,550 metres as the height at which the oxygen stopped working. (Compagnoni in his book wrote 'around 8,400 metres, perhaps higher'). Discussing why this might have happened before the expected time, Lacedelli

---

[*] Though it was Mario Lacedelli, Lino's nephew, while selecting the photos for this book, who noticed this detail.

concludes either that there was leakage from the bottles or that the enormous effort required by the two climbers because of their heavy loads resulted in the oxygen being used at a greater rate than predicted. Another possibility was that the mixers didn't function correctly at the very low temperatures that they encountered near the summit.

As regards the photos discovered by Marshall, Lacedelli says that the masks were worn despite the fact that the oxygen had already finished, so as to breathe air that was less cold and less dry. This reduced the pain in their throats and windpipes that breathing the poorly mixed oxygen and the dry, freezing air above 8,000 metres caused. Anyone who has experienced double-digit sub-zero temperatures in the mountains knows that the practice of breathing with the face covered, or with the hands cupped over the mouth, is normal, instinctive behaviour, even if it cuts down the air flow.

Following Lacedelli's positive judgement on Bonatti, and his understanding of the rigours of his and Mahdi's bivouac, it is hard to understand why, when he was under no pressure from Desio, he would lie about the oxygen running out. Perhaps to give greater value to the ascent? Today Lacedelli says 'if only it had lasted as far as the summit!' It should not be forgotten that renouncing the use of oxygen on mountains above 8,000 metres only became a trend in the 1980s with the expeditions of Messner. In the same way that free climbing (i.e. climbing without artificial aids) was not considered in the 1950s, climbing at that altitude without oxygen would have been unthinkable and certainly not something to boast about. It was generally agreed at that time that climbing above 8,500 metres without oxygen for any length of time would result in death. So when the official report was released, claiming that the feat had been accomplished without oxygen, this would not have increased its value within the mountaineering community. There remains the theory that reporting the oxygen running out was invented with the aim of discrediting Bonatti and supporting the claims of Nino Giglio. But this doesn't convince either, for the simple fact that even today, Lacedelli continues to state that the oxygen ran out before reaching the summit, while strongly defending Bonatti against the other accusations. What motive would Lacedelli have today in lying over this issue?

With the Judgement of Eight Thousand Metres

'Yes, but they are only theoretical calculations. At Base Camp Abram calculated that the German Dräger bottles that we were using should last ten hours. Possibly at 8,000 metres the Dräger might leak, or might last a shorter time. And then it's possible that we might have used more oxygen than we thought because of the altitude and the effort. Also, the mixture wasn't necessarily very precise.'

This is Lacedelli's cautious rebuttal of Bonatti's meticulous calculations on how long the three bottles carried by both Compagnoni and Lacedelli should have lasted. He has applied the same caution in dealing with another two of Bonatti's claims regarding the breathing apparatus. Firstly, the refusal to free themselves of the bottles once they had run out, and secondly the fact that Compagnoni was still wearing the mask on the summit, as confirmed by the photograph. To Bonatti these two issues implied that the oxygen could not have run out before the summit, again contradicting the official account of the summit climb. But whereas the difference over the timings of the start of the climb could be the result of a mistake, there can be no mistake over when the oxygen ran out. It is the difference between error and falsehood. And a falsehood over the oxygen, Bonatti reasons, equates to premeditation. According to Bonatti, the story of the oxygen was a fundamental leg in a deliberate, premeditated attempt to discredit him.

Although he has given full support to Bonatti over the bivouac, assuming part of the responsibility himself, though assigning the major part to Compagnoni, in this interview Lacedelli has also confirmed that the oxygen ran out before the summit, and he suggests Bonatti should be cautious in jumping to conclusions when dealing with men and mechanical apparatus at 8,000 metres, a height at which bottles, distributors and mixers, and also the thoughts and decisions made by climbers, operate in a different way to how they operate at lower elevations.

Support for this cautious approach can be found in a classic book of Himalayan mountaineering, *Everest: the West Ridge*, the story of the successful 1963 American expedition. The climbers used oxygen above about 7,200 metres, the Americans having equipment vastly superior to that available to the Italians in 1954,* having been developed from that used in the successful Swiss expedition to Everest in 1956.

The oxygen bottles, as far as can be judged from the expedition report, were lighter than those used by the Italians on K2, and delivered a much larger quantity of gas: they could also be regulated by a special tap (another difference from the Italian equipment), which could be set to deliver a flow of between 0 and 4 litres per minute. The masks had been redesigned by Thomas Hornbein, who did the final ascent with Willi Unsoeld. They were produced from a single piece of rubber, thereby reducing from six to one the number of valves required. The new mask could also be easily cleared of the ice formed from condensation. The oxygen set was a much more efficient piece of equipment than that used on K2, benefiting from ten years of experience in the Himalayas and Karakoram. Yet despite all the low altitude tests and the calculations, the equipment still gave unexpected results when used at high altitude. Above Camp V, which was at 8,300 metres, Willi Unsoeld is quoted as saying, 'Tom, my oxygen is hissing, even with the regulator turned off'. Unsoeld continues, 'For the next twenty minutes we screwed and unscrewed the regulators, checking valves for ice, but to no avail. The hiss continued.' The situation was not so different from that described by Lacedelli, in that it was possible that the oxygen bottles were supplying more oxygen than they should have done, thereby running out sooner than

---

* The Italians used an open circuit apparatus which used two types of bottles: one model was produced in Italy, the other, the Dräger bottle, manufactured in Germany. The open circuit system was an evolution of that used on Everest by the Swiss during their attempt in 1952, and by the British in 1953.

predicted. The Americans encountered the opposite problem as they reached the summit, which shows that precise calculations cannot be applied to oxygen bottles: 'Here I unloaded my first oxygen bottle though it was not quite empty. It had lasted ten hours, which obviously meant I was getting a lower flow than indicated by the regulator'.

When faced with empty oxygen bottles, it is clear that the Americans were just as irrational as Compagnoni and Lacedelli. Hornbein and Unsoeld met Barry Bishop and Lute Jerstad under the South Summit, as they were descending. At this point Hornbein's oxygen ran out again. Notwithstanding the empty bottle which weighed four and a half kilos, Hornbein, his mind befuddled because of the high altitude, chose not to remove it. 'Ought to dump the empty bottle, I thought, but it was too much trouble to take off my pack'.

This episode has echoes of Lacedelli's story in which, on account of his frozen hands, and thinking he was near the summit, he didn't remove the empty bottles and decided instead to carry them to the summit to leave there to confirm his arrival. Bonatti asked in his book why Lacedelli and Compagnoni had not abandoned the 'by now useless heavy containers. It must have been miserable transporting those heavy bottles to the bitter end, when logically it would have been easier to remove them'. It would seem that logic and ease do not readily apply to situations at 8,500 metres, resulting in actions incomprehensible to a cool mind at a low altitude. Reduced mental clarity would have made the idea of transporting the empty bottles more appealing than interrupting their 'robotic movements'. Bonatti, after his bivouac, should certainly have known better than most how different the world is up there.

Let us now return to the night the Americans had to spend at 8,535 metres on Everest in 1963 after they had been overtaken by darkness. Their situation was like Bonatti's: no oxygen, no tent or sleeping bags. The ordeal, reading Hornbein's account, resembled that of Bonatti and Mahdi, with the same problems: the undoing the buckles of the crampons, the massaging of dead fingers, the slowly passing time, the tremors which became spasms, and a drowsiness to be overcome at all cost. Hornbein's account is so enthralling that it is easy not to notice when he says, 'The oxygen was gone, but the masks helped a little for warmth.' So, with no oxygen left, the Americans continued to keep their masks on. Just as Lacedelli says Compagnoni did on the summit, and for the same reason. If someone had taken a photo of Hornbein and Unsoeld, maybe a Robert Marshall would have been able to lay finally to rest the story of the oxygen running out.

Erich Abram was the climber on the Italian 1954 team whose task it was to prepare and look after the oxygen bottles. Abram displayed a good technical grasp of the equipment, arising from his professional experience. I questioned him, the better to understand how the breathing set worked. Abram confirms that the three bottles were interconnected through isolating valves. As well as the bottles there was a space, or 'lung', in which the oxygen was mixed with air drawn from outside. At every breath a membrane and a valve operated so that the proportion of oxygen increased or decreased according to the intensity of the breath. There was a corrugated tube that connected the oxygen-enriched air to the mask. The mask was equipped with two valves that allowed breathing in and breathing out. This abridged system information is very important in several ways.

The first is that the duration of oxygen supply from the bottle is dependent on the intensity of the effort. If a greater effort requires heavier breathing, this will inevitably lead to a greater consumption of oxygen. We know that the final ascent was particularly tiring because of the effort (heavy oxygen bottles, 600 metres difference in altitude and difficult sections), and because of the elevation can therefore deduce that the duration of the oxygen would likely have been reduced.

The second concerns the possibility of continuing to breath without removing the mask, even when the oxygen has run out. The membrane and valve in the mixing space would have resulted in an interruption to the supply from the bottles but an increase in the external air supply, though at the cost of a greater resistance to breathing. According to Abram, once the oxygen had run out it would have been possible to continue breathing air via the mixing space, even without isolating the oxygen bottles. The two valves in the mask would have guaranteed an inflow of fresh air, avoiding stagnation with exhaled air. This proves that Compagnoni, with the oxygen mask still attached to his face at the summit, was perfectly capable of breathing, even after the oxygen had run out. The slim resistance caused by the membrane and valve would have made breathing more of an effort, but it would have been possible. Lacedelli notes that Compagnoni only put his mask on 'a few times' to humidify and warm up the air, probably because it wouldn't have been easy to breathe in this way for a long time and under exertion.

Certainly, when the oxygen ran out, both Compagnoni and Lacedelli would have noticed a sense of suffocation that would not have been reduced, as Marshall has written, simply by removing the masks. This problem was actually solved when Lacedelli and Compagnoni stopped and hyperventilated, not by removing their masks, this being more of a psychological reaction than a physiological one. Once on the summit, breathing through the mask should have been easier, since the two were no longer climbing. Abram also noted that, during the coldest and windiest days on the Abruzzi Spur, it was common for the mountaineers to climb with the mask on and the tube under the jacket, even without oxygen bottles. This illustrates that the problem of dry icy air was a real one and that there was a constant need to humidify and warm up the air for breathing. It should also be noted that the oxygen in the 1954 bottles was not the 'medical' grade used today: it was the same type of compressed oxygen used in bottles for welding. The inflammation and throat dryness caused by that oxygen resulted in a continuous discomfort.

So this brief analysis of the oxygen sets used on the 1954 K2 expedition disproves Robert Marshall's theory, seized on by Bonatti, that Compagnoni would not have kept the mask on once the oxygen had run out. Marshall was also mistaken when he insinuated that the photo of Compagnoni on the summit wearing the mask was excluded from the official photos in order to betray Bonatti. Marshall has written that the photo was substituted, in Desio's book, by 'a blurred photo, of inferior quality to that of Compagnoni with the mask', while the photo of Lacedelli in the book was used only because 'the ice on the beard was such a minor detail that it would not have prompted a casual observer to understand its significance'. The ice on the beard results, according to Marshall, from Lacedelli 'having just removed his mask'. If we are talking about a 'media plot' to remove the compromising photos from the public, it didn't work very well, from today's perspective. To find a photo of Compagnoni with the mask and Lacedelli with ice on his beard, there is no need to go to Australia and look in *Mountain World*. Those two same photos were published in *Corriere della Sera*, the largest-circulation Italian newspaper, in enlarged form, on the 28 September 1954 to illustrate an article by Cesco Tommaselli.

All this lends credibility to the account that the oxygen could have run out before the summit. The opinions of Lacedelli and Compagnoni differ on the height, but this appears of relatively little importance. As regards Robert Marshall's theory, Bonatti has no more need of it. Firstly, Lacedelli exonerates him completely from the charge of having used the oxygen himself. Secondly, Abram has explained that such an action would have been impossible. Without the mixer that Bonatti was lacking on the night of 30 July, the oxygen could not have been tapped in any way, even with a screwdriver.

Bonatti, Compagnoni and the Pakistanis

There was something which did not ring true when comparing what happened in the last few days of July 1954 and what appeared in Nino Giglio's articles. Giglio admitted during the libel trial of November 1966 that his sources were Compagnoni and Ata Ullah, the Pakistani liaison official who had gathered the complaints of the Hunza Mahdi. Mahdi also gave written evidence to the court in Turin. In the deposition he confirmed that he had been urged by Bonatti to accompany him to the summit for 'the honour of his country', but denied using the oxygen during the bivouac. It is curious that Compagnoni, who knew well that *all* the climbers used to treat the Hunza porters this way – as Lacedelli has stated in the interview – did not explain this to Giglio. It is also unlikely, given that Mahdi denied using the oxygen, and that Ata Ullah had taken his statement, that it could have been Ata Ullah who insisted the opposite. Thus the only possible source is Compagnoni. But why would Compagnoni tell Giglio a story he knew was false? Compagnoni knew that the masks were with himself and Lacedelli in the tent at Camp IX, so Bonatti would not have been able to use the oxygen. Unless he was suggesting that Bonatti had managed to release the oxygen by forcing the bottles in some way, the facts were undeniable, as Lacedelli agrees and has stated. So, why did Compagnoni not pour water on the flames that had been ignited by Nino Giglio?

According to Robert Marshall, Compagnoni actually poured petrol on the flames in order to exonerate himself. Marshall suggests that Compagnoni felt he was to blame for the frostbite and subsequent amputations suffered by Mahdi, and maintains that the fact that Mahdi had made public that Bonatti had coerced him into climbing with him gave Compagnoni the perfect opportunity to put the blame on to Bonatti for the frostbite. When, back in Karachi, the press later accused Compagnoni of having prevented Mahdi from reaching the summit, Desio, together with Ata Ullah, ensured a wall of silence was erected to avoid prejudicing the good relations between Italy and Pakistan. The Pakistani media were instead treated to the sanitised version of events prepared by the Italian Consul, Benedetto d'Acunzo. But, wrote Marshall, that left something smouldering under the surface.

In 1961 Bonatti published his autobiography, which naturally included his version of the events of that night. Compagnoni did not come out of it well. At that point Compagnoni, who could count on the support of Desio and Ata Ullah, dusted off the story that had come out in 1954, and found in Nino Giglio a useful and unexpected instrument of revenge. To counter Bonatti's argument that the oxygen had not actually run out, Compagnoni brought forward the time of departure and invented, according to Marshall, the story of the oxygen running out at 16.00, before reaching the summit. It was actually Compagnoni, claims Marshall, who was behind the accusations against Bonatti.

To recapitulate: the fear of being substituted by Bonatti provoked Compagnoni into moving the position of Camp IX; this decision resulted in Bonatti and Mahdi's bivouac; the bivouac resulted in Mahdi suffering serious frostbite which gave Compagnoni a strong sense of guilt; and the sense of guilt resulted in him shifting the blame on to Bonatti. We will close this chain of events at this point, but let us not forget that, according to Marshall, Compagnoni's desire to discredit Bonatti, which had not been achieved by the 'd'Acunzo report', found full satisfaction in Nino Giglio's columns.

Lacedelli, in a general sense, backs up the 'Marshall theory'. Bonatti's sacrifice appears plausible, though Lacedelli disagrees with Marshall on at least two points: he confirms that the oxygen did actually run out before the summit, and he denies strongly that there was any bad blood between himself and Bonatti over the Grand Capucin issue. But he also adds a worrying detail to support the theory of a plot against Bonatti: he remembers Compagnoni, during the fortieth anniversary celebration in 1994, saying 'Let's hope Mahdi doesn't say anything', to which Lacedelli asked for an explanation without being answered. What was Compagnoni worried about? What did he think Mahdi might confess? Perhaps that someone had put pressure on him, in 1954 or in 1965, to make a false declaration, or, at least, to avoid telling the truth? What was certain, remembers Lacedelli, was that 'Mahdi was well enough. He had been a bit down but now he was getting on okay. We spoke for a long time. He seemed really pleased to see us and he didn't say anything against anyone'. A completely different attitude from the one that would be expected of a porter with a grudge against the Westerners who had deceived him, denying him a chance of reaching the summit after having involved him in a plot against Lacedelli and Compagnoni, and leaving him with such serious mutilations.

The Motives of the State?

It has been suggested previously that the friendly relations between Italy and Pakistan resulted in a sanitised version of events, keeping all the arguments and embarrassments away from the public. However, it is not believable that the K2 expedition was the only reason for these friendly relations. To understand the true nature of the relationship between the two countries we need to take a step into the past and ask why Italy was granted permission for the expedition in the first place: the story that Ardito Desio's report on the Stak glacier swayed Pakistani opinion doesn't seem credible.

At that time K2 was not only 'The Italian Mountain' but was also 'The American Mountain', one they had attempted three times, failing to reach the summit by a whisker (Wiessner, 1939). It is not hard to imagine that, after their attempt in 1953, the Americans would have been keen to make another attempt in order to secure their position among the great mountaineering nations.

Many of those who knew Ardito Desio remember that he was pleased to have beaten the Americans, who had indeed sought permission for another expedition to K2 in 1954. In 1953, the year in which the application was made, Italy was a small country, still flat on its back after the Second World War. The USA, on the other hand, had become the most powerful military and economic power in the world. It seems improbable that Italy could have won the competition against the USA because of a simple report about a glacier.

It was certainly something else which made Mohammed Ali, the Prime Minister of Pakistan, decide in Italy's favour. We now know that the people involved in the negotiation for permission were Baron Scola-Camerini, head of the cabinet office of the Ministry of Foreign Affairs, Minister Canali, and the Italian Prime Minister himself, Alcide De Gasperi.

It is now necessary to make a small historical diversion. After the partition of India and Pakistan in 1947 the new borders were fixed. The frontier cut the great basin of the Indus in two, giving India the upper part of the river and its tributaries. Almost immediately, India began the construction of dams and canals that reduced the flow of water from the rivers Ravi, Sutlej and Beas, eastern tributaries of the Indus. This threatened cultivation of the land along the Pakistani part of the river, and resulted in a dispute between the two countries, which was not resolved until an agreement was signed in 1960 after long mediation by the United Nations and the World Bank. That agreement gave India the right to exploit the Beas, Ravi and Sutlej, tributaries of the Chenab, while Pakistan was granted the right to exploit the remaining waters of the Chenab, the Jhelum and the main course of the Indus.

As a result of the agreement from the beginning of the 1950s Pakistan had begun a series of monumental works in the Indus basin. These works attracted many Italian companies into Pakistan. Thanks to governmental finance and large loans from the World Bank, canals and other infrastructure projects were begun, and large dams were built at Kotri, Taunsa and Guddu. At the same time studies, projects and the granting of related contracts resulted in the World Bank approving the Tarbela dam project in 1965, the biggest project of its type in the world at the time. The construction of the dam, with the purpose of supplying, amongst other things, water to Rawalpindi, was assigned to a consortium of companies, among which the principal partner was the Italian company Impregilo.

Lacedelli confirms that he met employees of Italian construction companies from the day he arrived in Pakistan, Italians working in Karachi, Lahore and Rawalpindi. It is not possible to draw specific conclusions from this, but it is certainly fertile ground for further investigations. In his book on the K2 expedition, Ardito Desio wrote that De Gasperi met Mohammed Ali in Rome during a diplomatic visit which took place 'some time before' 15 July,* a visit during which De Gasperi pleaded the case for the expedition. There is no doubt about the meeting between Mohammed Ali and De Gasperi since the Pakistani Prime Minister referred to it in the letter he sent granting permission, reproduced in Desio's book and dated 27 July.

And yet this was not supposed to have been an 'official' visit. In *Corriere della Sera* for example, there was no mention of the meeting between the two statesmen. Forgetfulness can be excluded, since the *Corriere* at the time used to give great prominence to visits to Italy by foreign heads of government. In 1953, for example, it published photos and news about the official visit of the Princess of Tonga, and there was considerable publicity when the Pakistani Prime Minister made an official visit to India. Those who understand the subtle language of international diplomacy know that a visit which maintains a low profile can be kept unofficial, a useful ploy when the parties are discussing economic questions, or when they do not want certain other countries to be too well informed. Was it the Americans, also looking for permission to go to K2, who were not to know about the negotiations between Italy and Pakistan? What was discussed in this diplomatic encounter?

It would not be outrageous to suppose that the Italian government might have placed on the table a series of economic or commercial inducements in order to assist in gaining permission for the expedition. We should not be scandalised by this Realpolitik, demonstrating the Italian government's intention of regaining some presence on the international scene. On the contrary: we are not discussing a moral issue, we are painting a picture of the background to the expedition in order to explain why it was so important that friendly relations should not be risked on its return. If we could discover the economic, political and commercial discussions that took place in order to secure the expedition, the machinations between Desio, Ata Ullah and Compagnoni that Robert Marshall has referred to would be more understandable.

---

* In the *Diary of the Expedition*, published as an Appendix to his book, Desio suggests that the date was 19 June 1953.

Equally understandable would be the reason for paying so much attention to Pakistani public opinion, and the resulting false testimonies and plots. Perhaps one day we will discover that Bonatti was sacrificed, not only because of the pride and egotism of the authoritarian Ardito Desio, but also in order not to disturb higher interests – companies, contracts and economics – interests which could not be easily maintained in the face of fierce hostility from the Pakistani public against a group of callous Western mountaineers who took advantage of a proud Hunza, denying him the chance of reaching K2's summit and leaving him terribly mutilated. Perhaps we can now understand that the 'd'Acunzo report', the incomplete account which maintained the veil of silence, and the lies written about Walter Bonatti were actually a requirement of the Italian State, which, in 1954, needed both a sanitised version of events and a scapegoat.

If that is understood, then, finally, the fifty years of lies and hostility find a basis in a whole spectrum of reasons beyond those of personal character – the individual rivalries, jealousies and egotism that have, up to now, been assumed. The baseness of the human soul is not a sufficient motive to explain the mess that the story of the Italian K2 expedition became.

Until now, all we really have had are unofficial stories and the incomplete accounts of some individuals. Having listened to Lino Lacedelli provide a testimony fundamental to an understanding of what happened, we must now face up to a broader, more objective view. A view that does not change our admiration for an extraordinary mountaineering achievement, but cannot deflect our abhorrence of all the nastiness that accompanied it. Now, fifty years later, we can no longer ignore an objective account of the historic facts.

Conclusion: K2, a story for Everyone

'We are Europeans', we Italians occasionally tell ourselves, deluding ourselves that this is a solution to our national problems or a compensation for our lack of national pride. We are in Europe for economic stability, a result of a common currency and new laws, but certainly not for a common attitude towards history.

Let us consider the Germans, British and French. Their history, from the Second World War to the present time, is a story of revision and reinterpretation, carried out continually with a rigour and objectivity which seems almost masochistic to us. The historical debate in these countries has always involved universities, publishers and the media. There are no taboos, no chapters in their history that cannot be discussed. The accumulation of a historical perspective is continuous and intense, and enriches the collective life.

Things are different here. Italy is a strange country, a country in which, even today, we do not know precisely why in recent decades there have been explosions on trains and aeroplanes full of unsuspecting passengers, and in banks and railway stations packed with innocent people. A country that seems to deny its people an objective study of history before forty, fifty or sixty years have passed from the events in question. This has happened, taking examples at random, over the nerve gas we used in the colonial wars, our concentration camps in Yugoslavia, the partisan vendettas after the war, the massacre of Portella della Ginestra, the tragedy of Vajont. And it has happened again with the story of the K2 expedition of 1954. Of all the great mountaineering expeditions to the Himalayas and Karakoram, none has been as rich in controversy as ours. None has been so difficult, even today, to revisit. None has produced so many arguments, rivalries, and court cases.

Yet the information for an objective reassessment has been available. It had already been said or written, although occasionally it was necessary to look between the lines. To discover what was missing it would have been enough to question the witnesses. The problem is that nothing that has been said or written about K2 has ever been subjected to a rigorous historical interpretation, and most of the witnesses have never been questioned.

The only people who have been heard are those involved in the arguments, and then only when those arguments were actually in progress. As a consequence, it was not possible to get past the arguments.

This is a recurring problem in the way we Italians confront our recent past. Rarely do we consider history as an institutional or cultural question. On the contrary, we tend to think of it as a question of personal opinion, or worse, a private event of no concern to the general public. The consequence is that it is hard to make historical judgements, because these tend to be seen only as personal judgements. In order to write an account of the past, we have to wait until someone dies, someone forgets or someone loosens up. Only then, and with the blessing of the heirs, but still with the risk of being taken to court for libel, can we confront things.

Lacedelli is right when he says that telling the truth about K2 at the time would have been a waste of time. He would have been destroyed by Ardito Desio, who held a monopoly on the official story, secured by his rigid discipline of the other team members, and controlled the power of the media. If Lacedelli had tried to oppose Desio he would have ended up like Bonatti, an isolated, Don-Quixote figure, forlornly tilting at windmills.

It is sad that in the years since 1954 no one thought of collecting the stories of others involved in the events. Today, even a few minutes chat with Abram reveals the technicalities behind the oxygen apparatus, while a few hours discussion with Lino Lacedelli are enough to learn of the general climate in which the expedition took place, and to shed new light on many of the events that marked it.

Others should now take up the challenge of interviewing the remaining team members and exploring the diaries of those who are no longer with us. There is still the question of the relationship between Italy and Pakistan: this needs a more thorough investigation with a view to uncovering information that would allow us to go beyond the history of mountaineering, opening a window on the Italy of the early 1950s. What we require is a portrait of the Italian economy, of its media and of the institutions of the time. Everyone would profit from an understanding of the way in which a great adventure in the mountains integrated with a period in Italian life, now before the last threads of memory vanish.

That history should belong to everyone. For too many years we have been constrained to read about K2 only through the proceedings of civil and criminal court cases. For too long the story has been like a third-class thriller. But the real story had all the ingredients of an extraordinary adventure. A voyage of great exploration from another era, a story full of surprises, moments of ecstasy and profoundness, both good and bad.

We have wasted the opportunity for so much poetry and literature. Instead we have spent fifty years discussing Compagnoni's oxygen and Mahdi's fingers, Desio's book-keeping and the altitude of Camp IX. A 600-month gossip at 8,600 metres on the second highest mountain on the planet. What a waste! What a bore!

I say to the surviving K2 mountaineers – if the truth of your expedition has not appeared in these pages, then write it quickly. You are old and so are we, your humble contemporary spectators. Like you, we are no longer well. Write it quickly because, after the facts, after the necessary history, we would like to hear what you have to say about that huge sky, that place, so icy and so powerful, and about the eleven boys from the Italian mountains who found themselves one day on a mountain bigger than they could possibly have imagined. Take us up there. Tell us of your steps, your thoughts, without rhetoric, without rancour. Write for us as Melville wrote to Ned Bunn after a life spent on the far off oceans:

> *To us old lads some thoughts come home*
> *Who roamed the world young lads no more shall roam.*[*]

---

[*] From: 'John Marr and Other Sailors', Herman Melville, 1888.

124

Thanks

Lino Lacedelli and Giovanni Cenacchi thank Irene Pompanin who patiently transcribed the interview, and Alberta and Mario Lacedelli, guardian angels of this work. Mario Lacedelli in particular dedicated himself to this book with care, enthusiasm and generosity, which surpass everything one might expect from a family member and friend. Roberto Mantovani has been a constant point of reference for historical queries, while Erich Abram gave precious technical information. The authors' gratitude also goes to Pietro Crivellaro and Leonardo Lenti for their advice, to Luca Venchiarutti for the help given to this book, and to Roberto Condotta, Barbara and Cesare Morello, Graziella Accorsi and Giuseppe Savini. Without the affectionate intervention of our friend Mauro Corona, this work would not have found an outlet. Thank you also to Paola Lacedelli who supervised the English edition with generosity and competence.

Index